# Bittersweet Awakening

# Bittersweet Awakening

JO-ANN WASHINGTON

Printed in the United States of America

ISBN Paperback: 978-1983743023

LCCN: 201890077

Createspace independent publishing platform, North Charleston, SC

Interior Design: Ghislain Viau

*To the memory of my mother, Ruthine Hawley Cave,*
*Mr. and Mrs. Charles H. Barrett.*

*And to Mother Cabrini Home, which still provides residential*
*and educational services for neglected, abused,*
*and emotionally challenged children.*

# CONTENTS

# ACKNOWLEDGMENTS

This book would not have been possible without the encouragement, advice, and support of my dearest friends, Gloria J. Roebuck and Samuel E. Mosley, and my grandson, Joseph D. Barrett. Special thanks to Nancy P. Greenman for editing this book, understanding my intentions, and helping me improve my writing. In addition, love and gratitude to my three children, Ramon, Cleveland and Denise.

*The mother-child relationship is paradoxical and,
in a sense, tragic. It requires the most intense love on the mother's side,
yet this very love must help the child grow away from the mother,
and to become fully independent.*
—Erich Fromm

# PROLOGUE

### Letter To My Mother

Dear Mother,

For too long, my heart and mind were definitely not in sync, which is why I was unable to say these things to you sooner. I am sorry I did not speak or write these words to you many years ago. Perhaps you would have appreciated expressions of this nature more deeply if they had been made personally. Alas it took much prayer and deep thought for me to finally arrive at this point.

For years, I wrongly placed the onus of my negative feelings on you, but upon reflection, I realize that my emotions and actions are my own responsibility—not yours. The suffering you may have endured was more than likely overwhelming enough without my adding to it. My thoughts were always about me and how much

I hurt because of you, but I never gave thought or consideration to your feelings. I can imagine how you may have suffered quietly without ever telling me what you had endured before and after I was born. My actions or inactions throughout my teen years and as an adult could not have helped. Had I been aware of those intense issues that may have contributed to some of your unhappiness in life, I would like to think I would have made myself more available to you.

However, this inward journey allowed me to recognize the legitimacy of my feelings and the illegitimacy of my faults. Prior to this journey, I failed to realize that my anger was more with myself than with you. My bitterness was a result of stubbornness on my part for not allowing the possibility of you to be the mother I always wanted and dreamed of having. I regret never discussing my childhood with you nor telling you how I felt about it, and never asking you what determined the decisions you made. Last but not least, I regret not initiating communication.

My lack of in-depth understanding prevented me from reaching out to you while, at the same time, it fostered dislike and resentment toward you. I cannot believe I allowed that negativity to fester inside of me for so long. This journey has been like riding a roller coaster that at times I wanted to stop, but that I knew had to continue through all the rough peaks and valleys to eventually reach the calm.

Another of my faults was my unwillingness to forgive. For me, moving forward was not an option without forgiveness. The negativity imposed too heavy a burden. I should not have given that much credence to those particular circumstances that unfortunately resulted in strife between us. Although I have reached a calmer place and have forgiven myself for some of my faults, I do feel remorse for never having called you "Mother" or expressing the words "I love you."

I forgive you for what I thought was your inability to care for me when I was a child. And most of all, I forgive you for never having expressed physically or verbally that you loved me. It was unrealistic for me to have waited for you to do those things. As I look at my life retrospectively, I realize I could have given you the same unconditional love I wanted for myself.

Mother, I am sorry for not giving you the respect you deserved not only because of who you are but because of what you mean to me. I have never wanted any one in my life more than you. I foolishly abandoned the many available opportunities to make you aware of just how much I needed you in my life. You are the reason I exist. My inner strength is attributed to you and your ability to believe in something so strongly that you never allowed it to be penetrated or altered by anyone or anything regardless of the circumstances. Others may call it something else, but I call it strength. Whenever I set my mind to accomplish something, my inner strength kicks in, and there is no holding me back. Courage is another quality I attribute to you. It allows me the mental capacity to identify an idea or plan, pursue it, and persevere until I accomplish it.

Thank you for allowing me to learn lessons taught only by experience. I deeply apologize for not seeking your forgiveness before the sun set upon us for the final time.

Jo-Ann Washington

# PREFACE

As I look back on my relationship with my mother, I realize it had been strained from early in my life. Circumstances and conditions beyond my control led to periods of disappointment and uncertainty. I blamed my mother for leaving me at an early age—without ever knowing the situation or circumstances that prompted her decision. In addition, I blamed her for all the discontent and disillusionment I endured during my childhood, the main source of which was that I was an abandoned, motherless child.

As a child, I wanted my mother in my life more than anything or anyone else in the world, but that never happened. Even when we communicated as adults, my mother never told me why she was unable to care for me as a child. I carried that hurt around for many years. I didn't know if she could not afford to take care of me, was physically unable to take care of me, or did not want to take care of me. If she had opened up to me and explained the reason she had placed me at Sacred Heart, perhaps I could have accepted whatever it was. Knowing would have been better than not knowing.

At the time my mother probably did what she thought best for me, which was to place me in that facility. And in her mind, perhaps that was better than putting me up for adoption. Her decision made it possible to know in whose custody I was, where I was located, and to whom I really belonged. She could return to get me. That only happened when I was a teenager and no longer eligible to remain at Sacred Heart.

As an adult, I put a lot of thought and consideration into my childhood years—concluding that although I did not live with my mother nor was raised by her, I was never motherless. She may not have physically been in my presence, but she was always on my mind. It is troubling to me that I do not remember anything about her or anything else before the day she took me to Sacred Heart. Futilely, I have looked inward in hopes of discovering thoughts of anything that occurred in my life before that day. Also, I asked myself hundreds of times why my memory prior to that day is blank. I don't know if something traumatic happened to me that I wanted to forget—thereby erasing my memory. Or maybe I had been moved around so much early in my life that nothing had enough meaning for me to remember.

However, I remember everything about my mother quite distinctly the day she left me at Sacred Heart. I clearly remember what she wore and how she looked on that day. Her gray skirt and gray, waist-length, belted jacket looked so neat. The small pill-box hat she wore was that same gray color. Her short, black, curly hair hung loosely from under the hat, and the high-heeled shoes she wore were the same color as her hair. Although I remember everything about how she looked, I do not even remember the color of the dress or shoes I wore. My mother looked so beautiful, and her image from that day has always remained with me.

When I was younger, there was not a moment I did not wish to be with my mother—if only for a few minutes or to just see her face or watch her smoke a cigarette. When the opportunity became available for me to live with her, however, I neglected to take advantage of that precious time. I could possibly overlook some of my actions as a teenager by making excuses, such as *I did not know any better* or *a child does not think like an adult*. However, as an adult, there were no excuses for my actions or inactions toward my mother, nor were there reasons to justify my inappropriate behavior. I never forgave her for what I thought was her abandonment of me as a child. Those feelings of abandonment remained with me for too many years. I did try unsuccessfully to cover up my feelings. My actions or inactions spoke much louder than words ever would.

I never put myself in her position by trying to either understand how she felt or imagine what she was experiencing as a mother who was not treated as such by her only child. Would our relationship have been less strained if she had other children? When I was with her, she never gave me the impression that anything bothered her, and I tried to do the same. But it was hard for me to be in her presence without displaying my true feelings. She was my mother whom I loved, but I was unwilling to tell her. She deserved so much more from me.

Yes, I made myself available to assist her by performing menial tasks, such as helping her move, taking her to the store or doctor, or cleaning her apartment. But those things pale in comparison to saying the words that would have been most meaningful. For all those years,

I let my feelings dictate my actions and inactions instead of revealing what was truly in my heart. If I was subconsciously trying to punish or hurt my mother, it actually backfired. I hurt myself just as much—or more—because I deprived myself of the thing I wanted and needed most in my life, which was expression of my mother's love.

I can only imagine how we would have felt and reacted if I had hugged her, told her that I loved her, and explained how proud I was to be her daughter. Those heartfelt words coupled with my love would have enriched my life and, hopefully, her life as well. We could have had a strong mother-daughter relationship without the past overshadowing our lives; that powerful moment never came to fruition because of my stubbornness.

Life between us reminded me of a roller coaster with its ups, downs, twists, and turns. However, despite all of that, we had more in common than either of us realized. My mother went out of her way to help those in need, and I performed volunteer work. She loved to read and had many books in her home, as do I. She loved pets. I remember her having birds and a dog, and her last pet was a cat. My favorite pets were always dogs. Whenever I visited her, she had a pot of coffee on the stove. She drank coffee four or more times a day—and I also love coffee.

I must have gotten my creativity from her. She made braided rugs and quilts. She made a huge braided rug and several quilts for me, a quilt for each of her grandchildren, and for a few of her great-grandchildren. I asked her to write down the quilt-making instructions for me, which she did. But I have not yet tried to make one. In addition, I have her braided-rug instructions. I love to crochet blankets and afghans and used to sew my own clothes. My mother's favorite color was yellow, so I crocheted a reversible blanket for her bed. One side of the blanket was yellow, and the other side was brown. She had a big smile on her face the day I gave her that blanket.

We did differ in some ways. My mother really enjoyed country-western music, but I preferred rhythm and blues. One of her biggest enjoyments was listening to country-western music, which she knew I did not like. Many times when I visited, she was listening to the music and would increase the volume when I entered her door. I never complained. Whenever there was a country-western star performing in the area, she would attend the performance. Cigarettes and country-western music were her greatest pleasures.

Words are very powerful and meaningful when they are spoken from the heart and directly to the person for whom they are meant. Written words may have similar effect, but without human involvement, may convey less emotion. As I write this manuscript, I believe my words express my true feelings. If my mother could have read them and felt the emotion with which they were written, it might have been a shared bittersweet awakening.

# PART I

# EARLY CHILDHOOD

CHAPTER ONE

# ORPHANAGE

The first time I remember riding in a car, I was sitting between a dark-skinned man, who was driving, and my mother. I had no idea where we were going. My mother leaned over and folded my socks above my ankles, brushed the front of my dress, and then lit a cigarette. She sucked on the cigarette, turned her head toward the open window, and blew out smoke. As soon as she finished that cigarette, she lit another and then another.

The windshield framed the blue sky and its scattered clouds. That was all I could see. My mother mashed the remainder of her last cigarette in the ashtray when the car stopped. Once out of the car she reached for me without saying a word. She turned me around, straightened my dress, and wiped the corner of my mouth with her thumb. I guess when my appearance pleased her, she pulled down both sides of her skirt and adjusted the little hat she wore. There was stillness in the air.

As we walked hand in hand toward the building and up the stairs, I listened to the tapping of her high-heeled shoes on the concrete steps. When we reached the top, I noticed another set of identical steps on the opposite side of the platform. We stood in front of two huge, wooden doors, and she looked me over once again before she pressed the button. One door was opened by a strange-looking woman dressed in black from head to toe. My mother never entered the building but placed my hand into that of the odd-looking person.

"Be a good girl, and do what the sisters tell you to do," she said.

Those were the only words she said before I was led away. I turned back in her direction, but all was blurred.

My new home was Sacred Heart Orphanage Asylum, located on approximately four hundred acres of land that overlooked the Hudson River in West Park, New York. It was owned and operated by the Sisters of the Sacred Heart of Jesus. The home would later be renamed Mother Cabrini after its founder Francis Xavier Cabrini.

There was also a convent on the premises somewhat removed from the rest of the buildings and surrounded by a tall brick wall. The nuns never spoke to us about it, but we heard that was the place where young Catholic women, who were called novices, studied and prepared to become nuns. We could tell the novices from the nuns because, although they wore ankle-length habits, they were dressed in white from head to toe. Their hair was visible under a white veil. Once the novices became nuns, their outfits changed, and they dressed the same as the nuns with their hair totally covered. We were told by the nuns that we were not allowed to talk to the novices when we saw them on their way to or from church.

Girls residing in the home ranged from three to fourteen years of age and were separated into four different groups. The "babies," who ranged in age from three to five, resided in a separate building. Girls aged six to eight were called "little girls," those aged nine to eleven were "middle girls," and "big girls" were aged twelve to fourteen. The dormitories, dining rooms, and playrooms were separated according to those groups. Visible separation was evident while attending church. Each group was assigned two nuns as their overseers every day except when in school. All dormitories for the girls were located on separate floors in the same building. The racial makeup of the girls residing at the home was black, Latina, and white.

Sister Augustina, a short, stocky woman who wore glasses and lacked any distinguishable feminine features, was one of the sisters assigned to the middle girls. Her furrowed brows and dark circles around her eyes made her look tired and weary. Sister Gertrude, also assigned to the middle girls, was much thinner than Sister Augustina. She, too, wore glasses, and her parchment-like skin made her look much older. Sister Gertrude did not say much. All she did was look at us with her piercing stare to convey what she wanted. Each nun slept in an enclosed wood-paneled cubical at opposite ends of the girls' dormitory. Sister Augustina's corner cubical was located in the front section of the dormitory. On more than one occasion when one cubical was ajar I peeked inside. I only caught sight of a bed and small stand. There was no closet visible. Next to Sister Gertrude's cubical was a separate bathroom with tub, sink, and toilet that the nuns shared.

The spacious, high-ceilinged dormitories had approximately sixty beds divided by a wooden partition with two open walkways. Early every morning Sister Augustina rang a bell to wake us up. I was one who had the covers pulled off me or my ear pinched many mornings because I did not get out of bed when most of the other girls did. The girls in the front half would make their way to the washroom, which contained a long sink with faucets on both sides of a metal pipe running its length. Each girl was assigned a numbered, wooden cupboard that held a cup, toothbrush, and a comb placed in the bristles of a hair brush. The wooden fixtures decorated the walls and were separated by three huge windows. Underneath the cupboards were hooks that held our washcloths and towels. Toilet stalls and bathtub stalls were located on the windowless side of the room.

Our morning routine was to wash our faces and hands, comb and brush our hair, and brush our teeth. Those of us whose hair was braided did not comb or brush it daily. Sometimes we would help each other with the braiding. When we finished, we dressed with clothes kept in lockers outside of the washroom. While the first group of girls was in the washroom, others were making up their beds. The second group replaced the first, going through the same routine—followed by the other two groups. Nightgowns had to be folded and placed under pillows. We sat in chairs in the locker room, which had a television, until everyone was finished. We were not allowed to watch television unless the nuns deemed it appropriate, and it was never appropriate in the morning. When everyone finished getting ready, Sister Augustina inspected us to make sure we and our beds were presentable. Then we formed a single line for the walk to morning mass. We walked to church in our groups, and when mass was over, we lined up again for breakfast in four separate dining rooms—one for each group of girls. There was a long hallway with glass-topped wooden partitions separating two dining rooms per side.

After breakfast, some of the middle girls and big girls did assigned chores, such as clearing dishes, silverware, and glasses from the tables. There was never a dish with food left on it. We had to eat every bit of food in our bowl or on our plate even if we did not like what was served. When certain disliked food was served, some girls would give it to others—or negotiate a future trade. Others girls cleaned tables, inverted chairs on tables, and swept floors.

The dining room floors and hallway were mopped daily but only waxed and machine buffed on the weekend. Some girls were assigned to kitchen duty, where they loaded and unloaded the washing machine. Sister Eleanor, the short, robust nun in charge of the kitchen, did most of the cooking. Many of us were afraid of her because she was a strict disciplinarian who said what she meant and meant what she said. She gave orders but never a smile. Her presence invoked fear; when she was around, we did not talk, smile, or even whisper. If we were talking or joking around in the kitchen, our smiles faded when she entered the room. The only sounds heard were those of the dishes and silverware clacking together.

Some girls were assigned to clean the dormitories and washrooms. The hardwood floors were dust mopped, and, on weekends, waxed by hand and shined by foot. We applied the wax to folded, thick cloths and spread it on the floor in a circular motion while on our knees. When the wax dried, we folded another thick cloth and placed it under the right foot, moving it back and forth as we maneuvered our way down the aisle with the left foot. We would shine down the aisle one way and then turn around and go back in the opposite direction. Sometimes we had contests to see which aisles of the dormitory were the shiniest or who finished first. When they were not praying, the nuns had chores too. Some of us also worked in the laundry room. Although laundry was done every day, the girls only assisted on weekends.

Once chores were completed, we went downstairs to the locker room, which sometimes doubled as a playroom, where we changed into our school clothes. Different grades wore different colors. All of us wore brown skirts, but the blouses were pink, yellow, blue, or green. We all wore white socks and brown shoes. Before going to our classrooms, we assembled in the auditorium, where we prayed, pledged allegiance to the flag, and sang some songs from our song-books. The last song, which we always sang as we marched around and out of the auditorium, was the "Battle Hymn of the Republic." From there, we went directly to our classrooms.

Sister Christina was the pianist-organist who played for assembly, church services, and other functions. She was tall and slender, with a freckled face and big, blue eyes. Her nose was slightly slanted to the right. Sister Christina looked to be much younger than the other nuns. She was pigeon-toed, and when she walked, her long strides made her look as if she were gliding across the floor. We wondered why she had become a nun, because she was so pretty compared to the other nuns, who looked old, fat, rugged, and tired.

After eating lunch and doing kitchen and dining-room chores, we were allowed to play on the playground. Those who did not have chores played outside—weather permitting—or in the playrooms until it was time to line up and return to school. Sometimes we returned to church before going to the classroom. There was always a reason we had to attend church, especially during the month of May, when it seemed we were in church three times a day. When school was out, we changed clothes, played, and prepared for dinner. After dinner, we played some more until time to prepare for bed.

The first few years at the home were uneventful for me; I do not remember anything specific about that time period. For me, that time was spent becoming acclimated and conforming to all the rules.

Instead of being afraid of the way the nuns looked, we made fun of them. We also discussed ways to look under their long black garments, but we never could come up with a tactic that actually worked. The way they dressed and looked was strange to me.

They seemed to be mad all the time. Whenever they told us to do something, it was an order or command in a raised voice. If we did not move fast enough for them, they would scold us, push us, or hit us. Maybe they treated us that way because they were tired and were responsible for too many girls. The nuns always looked tired. Sister Christina was the only nun who smiled whenever we saw her.

We wondered if the nuns never looked happy because of protocol or perhaps a penance. Maybe they were not allowed to show any type of joy or happiness. Their facial expressions could have been a result of all those hours of hard work and prayer. We never saw them do anything else. When they were not working, they were praying—and they probably prayed while they worked. At least the girls, in addition to work and prayer, were given playtime—which made us happy—but we never saw the nuns play. Although many of us were sad at times, playing let us forget about whatever it was that bothered us. Many of us probably would have developed mental disorders if our entire daily regime consisted only of work and prayer.

We learned that the novices who lived in the convent would eventually become nuns. They all looked young and pretty. Sometimes we would sneak to the convent to be nosy, but we could not see anything because of the tall brick wall that surrounded the place.

I often wondered if they ever saw us sneaking around. Nothing was ever said to us about snooping, so if they had seen us, it was not mentioned to Mother Superior or any of the other nuns.

Somehow we learned that their ceremony to become nuns was very secretive, and none of us girls was allowed to watch it. We heard that the ceremony was to include the novices getting married to God. The secrecy surrounding that ceremony made it intriguing to us. We wondered why we were not allowed to watch it. We had to attend church every day anyway—sometimes more than once, especially on holy days, or for whatever other occasion deemed necessary. We decided to sneak into the church balcony to watch what we could of the ceremony. Some of the girls who did not join us told us that God would punish us for doing such things, but we did it anyway.

We knew that if the nuns had seen us in the church, we would have been punished. Luck was on our side, because we were never caught. We actually thought we would get a chance to see God during these ceremonies, but it never happened. We had no plan as to what we would have done or said if we had seen Him. We definitely would not have lied about what we were doing and why. Silently we watched the novices and the priest—all the while hoping we would get a glimpse of God—not realizing He was glimpsing us the whole time.

*Sacred heart orphanage asylum*

*Sacred heart orphanage asylum grounds in front of entrance*

CHAPTER TWO

# INSPECTION

One morning when I was six or seven years old, I got out of bed before the morning bell, quietly tiptoed to my locker, removed my clothes, and went directly to the washroom. As I reached the washroom, I noticed a pair of feet under one of the stalls, so I quickly entered another stall and remained there until I heard the other girl leave. I left the stall and stood at the side of the sink, where I would not be seen if someone entered the room. My hands shook as I shivered and turned the faucet on to a trickle. After washing myself and brushing my teeth, I dressed and quietly tiptoed back to my bed—hoping the hardwood floor would cooperate. Reaching my bed with a sigh of relief, I sat on the floor for several minutes and listened to strange sounds before deciding to make up my bed. Once that was done, I sat back down on the floor to avoid attention if anyone woke.

Judy, who was in the bed next to mine, turned over and saw me. "Jo-Ann, what are you doing? Why are you sitting on the floor?" she whispered.

"Shush, somebody's going to hear you," I said. "Go back to sleep." At that moment I thought maybe I had better go back to the washroom until the morning bell rang.

"Are you going to run away?"

"No. Now go back to sleep," I whispered, hoping there was no one awake to hear what she had said. Judy mumbled something as she turned away, pulling her covers around her neck. She was so nosey. Her sister Connie's, bed was on the other side of mine. Connie was a year younger than Judy. I sat with my arms folded and my hands tucked one over the other. At that moment, I was thinking about running away before anyone got out of bed, but I did not want to go alone. Some of us had previously talked about running away, but that morning I wanted to do so more than before. Had I run away, my absence would have been discovered at morning inspection. One thing of which I was certain: When we did run away, Judy would not be going with us. She could not keep a secret.

When I heard movement from Sister Augustina's cubicle, I knew it was time to hide. The washroom was the most logical place. If Sister Augustina heard anyone walking during the night, she would call out to ask who was up. There was no choice but to answer her. I held my breath as I tiptoed past the nun's cubicle. When I reached the washroom and entered one of the bathtub stalls, I let out a deep breath. I wondered how I could have been out of breath from tiptoeing. There was no better hiding place, because we never bathed in the morning. I waited in the stall until the other girls were getting ready for the day. When the first group was dressing, combing their hair, and brushing their teeth, I sneaked out of the stall without being noticed.

Sister Augustina's inspection included slowly walking through the aisles and glancing from side to side without saying a word. She would stop at someone's bed and point to a pillow or blanket or to untied shoes. Sometimes she even pulled the covers off the bed if it had not been properly made up. Before I realized her location, she had already begun to walk down my aisle. I turned to look at my pillow and then checked to see if my shoes were tied.

While I was thinking about why we had to go through that routine every morning, I noticed a pair of shoes suddenly appear at the foot of my bed. I looked up in time to see her glance at the row across from mine, and the reflection from the sunlight on her face added a smidgen of tenderness. Once her face turned in my direction I lowered my head and noticed that the corner of my blanket was not tucked under the mattress. How had I missed that? I thought I had checked everything. My heart was beating fast, and my hands shook beside me. I felt her stare before I noticed the black shoes move toward me. I had been up before everybody else and had more time to get ready than the other girls.

Once I realized she had seen the untucked blanket, I hurried to tuck it under, but was too late. Sister Augustina had pulled the entire blanket and sheet off my bed, allowing the strange aroma to flow throughout the area. My embarrassment and humiliation should have been enough punishment, but not for Sister Augustina. She had to let everyone know, not only by pulling the covers off the bed but also by holding my wet nightgown in the air so that everyone could see it before she threw it onto the wet circle on my bed.

Tears welled in my eyes. At that instant I attempted to run, but I was stopped by a tug of my braid, and then I felt that terrible pain of my ear being pinched.

"Stop!" I cried.

Sister Augustina ignored my cries and continued to pinch and pull my ear. My ear felt as if it were being torn from my head. I danced in circles on the tip of my toes in an attempt to lessen the pain.

"Leave me alone!" I cried.

"Be quiet!" she shouted.

The louder I cried and shouted, the harder she pulled and jerked. I tugged at her arm—begging her to stop. We continued to tussle. I tried to stick my foot out in an attempt to trip her, but that did not work. If I spun faster, she would get dizzy, I thought. It seemed as if we had spun in rhythmic movements for hours, but it had only been a few minutes before she began to breathe hard and loosen her grip. With that sudden ease of pain, I opened my eyes and saw what looked like a giant red tomato with raccoon eyes rapidly huffing and puffing. Girls stood in the aisles, knelt, and stood on beds as they tried to get the perfect view, not realizing they were blocking my escape route. At that moment the dormitory seemed so small, and all I could hear were her grunts and my cries.

When she finally let go of my ear, all the girls hurriedly straightened up their beds and themselves and stood to attention. Still breathing hard, Sister Augustina yelled, "Take those wet sheets and blanket to the laundry chute right now!"

The laundry chute was located immediately to the right upon entering the washroom. We would put our dirty clothes in the chute, where they rolled down through a long metal tube and would end in the laundry located in the basement. In my attempt to hurry to the laundry chute, I tripped on the bedding and heard whispers and giggles.

"That's enough!" Sister Augustina shouted.

When I reached the laundry chute, I opened the door, bundled the blanket and sheets together, pushed them inside with my nightgown, and listened as they swished through the chute to their destination below. Once I could no longer hear that sound, I closed the door, stood there, and cried uncontrollably.

I did not want to walk back into that room—not with all those eyes staring and the giggles, whispers, and snickers erupting. I cupped my hands over my face and hoped that would muffle my cries. That did not work, so I entered one of the bathroom stalls, which did not help much, either. There was a mixture of snot and tears in my hands when I reached for the toilet paper. I wiped my nose and eyes but continued to cry.

"Jo-Ann, Sister Augustina wants you back in the room," I heard between my sniffles.

I blew my nose and wiped my eyes again before opening the door.

"Why didn't you tell me what happened? I could have helped you," Judy said. "You could have thrown your wet sheets down the chute, and I would have given you one of mine."

Tears rolled down my face again when she said those words. "I was too scared to say anything," I replied.

"We had better go back into the room before Sister Augustina comes," Judy said as she took my hand and led me back into the room. I followed with my head down until I reached my bed, and then I cautiously scanned the room for Sister Augustina. Once our eyes met, I quickly lowered my head. She continued her inspection.

"Get in line," she ordered when finished with the inspection. We stood in the aisle at the foot of our beds, turned toward the door, and left the dormitory by row, in single file to church.

"Judy, did Sister Augustina tell you to come to the washroom to get me?" I whispered as we walked to church.

"No. I told Sister Augustina that I had to use the washroom," Judy said. From that moment, Judy was my best friend.

There were no whispers or passing notes in church that morning. Mass was recited in Latin, and I do not think any of us knew what we were saying. I never understood why Latin was not a subject taught to us in school. For the rest of that day and several days after, the only girl with whom I spoke was Judy. I did my chores and separated myself from others during play periods in the playroom or on the playground. In the playroom, I sat on a bench and made doll clothes with the material, needle, and thread given to those of us who wanted to sew. The girls who were not making doll clothes played jacks or other games or read books. I kept to myself for about two days.

CHAPTER THREE

# QUEEN BEE

Sunday was the saddest day of the week for me, because that was visiting day. I remember receiving only one visit from my mother. During that visit, I introduced her to Connie and Judy. When the weather was good, those of us without visitors sat on benches or swings to watch the girls with visitors. Sometimes I cried when I saw them and wondered why my mother had not come to visit me again. I felt anger toward her for leaving me at that place. And even though I did not know my father, I was angry with him too. My anger began to consume me so much that it resulted in my talking back to the nuns and getting into arguments and fights with the girls. I guess acting out was my way of getting attention. It was on a Sunday afternoon while on the playground watching girls with visitors that I decided to run away. Girls always talked about running away, but none ever did.

I decided to be the first. During one of our play periods, I recruited an escape party.

Saturday was the day to wax and shine the dormitory floor. We dust mopped the floor first. One particular Saturday when I had just completed dust mopping, Sister Augustina approached me and pointed to dust under one of the beds.

She said, "There is still dust on the floor; dust mop the entire floor again."

She stood so close while she scolded me that a whiff of her breath floated into my nostrils. It smelled like nothing I had ever smelled before, and I held my nose and said, "Get out of my face! Your breath stinks!"

She pulled the dust mop from my hands—the mop portion landing on my head. I do not know what came over me that day. I had never before spoken to any of the nuns in that manner.

After that incident, my punishment was isolation. I was moved to the medical area, separating me from the other girls. The only time I spent with them was during school. For church I had to sit in the balcony with some of the nuns and Sister Christina playing the organ. I slept and ate alone. My reaction to this punishment was to refrain from eating and participating in class. The nuns did not communicate with us anyway, unless it was to tell us what to do or what not to do. After four or five days of isolation, I returned to the dormitory.

I heard a loud, "Hi, Jo-Ann," when I returned to the dormitory. They were curious about my punishment. I had been returned to my bed between Judy and Connie. They informed me of the various things I had missed, such as who had gotten into trouble—and why. Everything else continued as usual, and my thoughts of running away had intensified.

Often Judy and Connie shared with me treats brought by their visitors. Their kindness slowly changed my way of acting with the other girls, but I still longed for attention. I got some by excelling in roller-skating. There was a paved roadway between the dining rooms and dormitory building and the playground that ended at a stone wall; we used it for roller-skating. We would have races down that road. The stone wall started at the gate entrance to the property and ran down the hill where we rode our sleds.

Behind the stone wall were huge walnut trees. We threw rocks at the walnuts to knock them down from the trees. When we determined we had enough walnuts, we would put them on the stone wall and crack open the thick, green covering with a rock. We had to remove the covering before we could crack open the nut. The green would stain our fingers and hands, but that did not deter us from enjoying our booty. For some reason, we felt as if those of us with the greener fingers were the most fulfilled. Usually those of us with green fingers and hands were the ones who got into trouble. The nuns had ordered us to leave those trees alone but they granted permission to eat only those nuts we found on the ground. We disobeyed. Often when the rocks we threw at the trees rained back down on us, we wished we had obeyed.

One day, thinking I could get to the walnuts faster, I decided to climb a tree, but I was unable to climb close enough to reach the nuts. On my way down from the tree, one of the branches seemed to grab my leg as I jumped. When I landed on the ground, I could see white skin before the blood began to gush out. I was taken to a hospital, and my thigh was stitched up. That incident ended my tree-climbing adventures.

The grapevine tunnel also lured us to adventures. It was a metal-framed tunnel with grapevines growing all around it. Those purple grapes were big, sweet, and juicy. The grapevine tunnel was in the opposite direction from the walnut trees. We were told not to eat any of the grapes when we walked through that beautiful and delicious tunnel, but we always did. We thought there was a nun assigned to watching the tunnel, because we always were caught picking grapes. Whenever someone was caught, her punishment was no dessert at our dinner meal. In addition to walnut trees and grapevines, there was an apple orchard, but since the apple orchard was too far from the playgrounds, we very seldom picked apples.

For amusement, we sometimes competed against each other playing jacks, sewing, or telling stories. I would win at jacks most of the time. When the weather permitted, we played outside and competed against each other in kickball, softball, hopscotch, war, roller-skating, and jumping double Dutch. Sometimes we would see who could swing the highest or who could swing and then jump farthest from the swing. Most of the girls wanted to be on my team because I excelled in sports and my team won most of the time.

Academics was another of my strong points. One of my favorite subjects was spelling, and on several occasions, I won spelling bees. In the classroom, we were divided into two teams to stand on opposite sides of the room. The teacher would give us words, alternating sides. The person who won would be given the prize: a statue of a holy figure. My first prize was a statue of the Virgin Mary. I was very proud of that statue because it was the first thing I had ever won.

Poetry also was one of my favorite subjects. In class, we had a poetry book from which we recited poems by Henry Wadsworth Longfellow, Edgar Allen Poe, and others. My enjoyment of poetry was the reason I would write articles and poems for the school newsletter, *Echoes*.

The playroom was a huge open room with built-in wooden benches against the walls. Next to the playroom was a washroom with long sinks and toilet stalls, and next to that was the locker room, where we kept our coats, leggings, hats, rubbers, and gloves. During bad weather, we would have to play inside and would sometimes take turns telling stories. We sat on the playroom floor in a large circle. I certainly delighted in storytelling, and I made up adventures that kept everyone in suspense. I could draw out a story for several days. Girls would offer to do my chores or give me their dessert to hear the story's mystery solution. I loved when I had captured everyone's attention telling a story. Their show of emotions when listening to my stories filled me with excitement and a sense of accomplishment.

I sat thinking deeply, allowing no interruptions before telling my story. At times, the nuns would even listen to me or one of the other girls tell their stories. The nuns eventually gave me the nickname Queen Bee, because I was always surrounded by a large following. I found a way to fill the void of my mother's inattention by acquiring friends.

With the difficult times during my childhood, friends meant the world to me. They always have had a special place in my heart, and enabled me to cope. I do not know what kind of person I would have become without their kindness and support. They listened to my rants and complaints—often when they probably did not want to do so. They laughed and cried with me and for me. They shared my sadness and pain, but they also shared some of my joy and happiness.

As a child at Sacred Heart, I would cry under my covers so that no one would hear me, only to find out later that my cries were indeed heard. Even at our young age, my friends knew the pain I felt and allowed me those private moments to release some of my feelings. Often when I saw girls with their visitors, I could not hold back my anger and tears. They listened to me and tried to comfort me as best as one child could do for another. We enjoyed lots of laughs when we competed against each other playing games or sharing stories.

The nickname given to me by the nuns didn't go unnoticed. It made me feel important—a leader. If they had realized how important being called Queen Bee meant to me and how it affected the others, the nuns probably never would have called me that. I enjoyed their recognition along with the added attention it prompted from the other girls.

One day I decided I wanted pierced ears, because I had noticed that most of the girls of Hispanic origin had pierced ears and wore cute earrings. I asked Maria to show me how to pierce my ears, and she guided me through the process. First, I threaded a needle with white thread. Colored thread could not be used. I don't remember how or where we got matches, but that was what we used to sterilize the needle. I rubbed my earlobe until it felt numb, held and stuck the needle in, and pulled the thread through it. I cut the thread and made a knot, allowing the thread to remain in my ear. Every day for a couple weeks I had to rotate the thread.

After weeks of rotating the thread, it was pulled out. A short piece of straw was burned on both ends and was put in my ear to replace the thread. The straw remained in my ear for several weeks before being removed. When the straw was removed, it was ready to be replaced with earrings. I didn't have a pair of earrings, so one of the other girls let me borrow her earrings in exchange for giving her my dessert for a few days, performing chores, or whatever else I could barter. Bartering with different girls enabled me to regularly wear earrings.

Also there was a time when I had a big white wart on my right elbow, and Evelyn told me that she knew how to take it off. She tied a piece of thread around the wart. Each day for several weeks, she tightened the thread. One day we were doing backflips, which was when two girls stood back to back, locked arms at the elbows, and jumped backward over the other. After I flipped over Evelyn's back, she noticed that my elbow was bleeding. I saw a lot of blood in the spot where the wart had been. If other girls had warts, I didn't notice anyone walking around with thread tied to their extremities.

I enjoyed being the leader of ear piercing, storytelling, or games we played but being the leader of bloody wart removals was not wanted.

*Mother and Jo-Ann on the grounds of sacred heart orphan asylum*

*Judy (L), Jo-Ann (C), Connie (R)*

## CHAPTER FOUR

# THOUGHTS OF RUNNING AWAY

One afternoon in the playroom with Judy and Connie, I decided to tell a story.

"Let's sit on the floor," I said.

"Are we going to play jacks?" Judy asked.

"No. I am going to tell a story." I saw Alice and Blanca sitting on the bench across from us. "Come over here," I said as I motioned for them to join us.

"What do you want?" Alice asked.

"Come sit with us. I am going to tell a story."

They joined us, completing the circle. I always started my stories the same way: "Once upon a time." Most of us began our stories with those words. As we sat in the circle, I hesitated for a few minutes with my head down in thought, but I already knew what my story would be about.

"Once upon a time, there were five friends who lived in a home with many other girls, and they were very, very sad. They did not like living there, so they decided to run away," I began.

I knew Connie and Judy were homesick, because they always talked about wanting to go back home with their mother and baby sister. Also, I knew that Alice and some of the others had previously talked about running away. The time could not have been better to tell that story. I finished telling the story before our play period was over.

"What would we need to do before we could run away?" Judy asked looking surprised. "Are you serious?" Connie asked.

"Hush, don't talk so loud," I said. "What do you think about us running away?"

"I always wanted to run away," said Alice.

Blanca perked up. "Me too," she said.

"Well, I don't know..." said Judy.

Connie said, "I'll go if Judy goes."

"You and Judy think about it for a few days and let us know," I said. Judy and Connie looked at each other and shook their heads in agreement.

"OK, now let's play jacks," Alice said.

"Who is first?" asked Connie.

Alice smiled as she said, "Since I suggested it, I'm first."

We played jacks until playtime was over.

While in bed a few nights later, I heard my name and turned toward the sound. "What?" I said.

But what I heard was, "Who is talking out there?" coming from Sister Augustina's cubicle.

We lay still and silent for a moment, hoping she would not get up. Sometimes when she heard girls talking or whispering, she would come out of her cubicle and walk the aisles. Judy decided we had waited long enough, so she held her covers over her head and whispered through a small opening, "We want to go with you."

I leaned from my bed. "What did you say?"

"Connie and I want to go with you."

I leaned farther. "Are you sure?"

"Yes," she said.

"Will Connie keep our secret?"

"I told her not to say anything to anybody. She will keep our secret."

"OK. Let's talk about it tomorrow," I said. With a sigh of relief and a smile on my face, I pulled the covers over my shoulders. "Good night, Judy," I said to her. I knew that was the beginning of an exciting adventure.

The next day while in the playroom, Maria came to where I was playing jacks and whispered in my ear, "We need to start making plans."

"OK. You go get Blanca, and Judy will get Connie."

We sat quietly in our storytelling circle and looked at each other. I was thinking about what I would say when Alice asked, "Where are we going?"

"I don't know. But any place is better than here. The nuns are always telling us what to do," I said.

Alice threw her head to one side, moving her thick black hair from her face. "We need to know where we are going," she said wisely.

"Route Nine is outside these gates. None of us knows what is around here. We have only walked up or down the mountain. There is nothing up the mountain but that shrine. We do know that the Hudson River and railroad tracks are down the mountain," I said.

"Then we should go down the mountain," Judy said.

"I agree. We can't go on Route Nine, because we would be spotted right away," said Connie.

"No one would expect us to go down the mountain. We need to go down the mountain toward the river. Who will look for us there? We can go where the river leads us," I said.

"When?" asked Judy.

"I am not sure when," I said, "but before we go anywhere, we need to start saving our cookies, candy, and fruit so that we will have something to eat."

"We don't get cookies and candy every day. And we have to eat our fruit at the table. So how can we do it?" Judy asked.

"We can hide the hard fruit in our clothes, bring it down here, and put it in our lockers. The other fruit we have to eat at the table. Save any goodies you may receive from a visitor, and put them in your locker," I replied.

"Why don't we wait until the summer? There's too much snow outside, and it's cold," Blanca complained. I was glad Blanca finally said something. Before that, she had just sat and listened to everyone else talk.

"That's a good idea. Let's wait," replied Connie.

"Why should we wait?" I said. "I think it is better to do it now. During the summer, everyone is outside at the same time with both nuns. Now some of us are inside with one nun and others outside with the other. That makes it easier for us to get away. We can go outside

32

and then say we are cold and want to come inside, but instead we can sneak away. If we are inside and get permission to go outside, we can leave. Both ways we can be gone before they notice we are missing."

We continued to perform our daily activities and save the food-stuffs we needed for our journey.

CHAPTER FIVE

# THE GREAT ESCAPE

One afternoon while pulling our sleds up the hill, Judy pointed to a good place behind the dormitory. The sloped cemented section behind the building was a good hiding place. No one would see us down there.

"That is the place where we should meet before we run away," she said.

When we reached the top of the hill, I said, "We've saved enough snacks for our journey, so let's tell the others that the next time we are allowed to play outside, we will escape."

It seemed forever, but that day finally came. We were outside playing, and one by one, we asked to go to the washroom and went to our lockers to get our snacks. We hid them under the top part of our leggings. Once back outside, we went to our meeting place, where we remained until everyone went inside. That was the beginning of our great adventure.

We traced our way down the hill swiftly until the deep snow slowed us down. The river was about four miles from the dormitory, but it seemed so much farther that day. Our heavy clothes and rubbers made it difficult for us to maneuver in the snow. Connie tried to skip but was soon out of breath. She should have known it was impossible to skip in the deep snow. Several times I looked back to see the building lights fade in the distance.

"We should have ridden the sleds down here. It would have been faster," Alice said.

We arrived at the river's edge and saw large blocks of ice.

"Jo-Ann, now what are we going to do?" asked Judy.

"We're going to get on the ice and ride it to wherever it takes us," I said as if I knew what I was talking about.

At that time we were all too ignorant of the dangers. My faith rode on a chunk of ice that could have been washed away by one misstep. Large blocks of ice were at the water's edge, so being the leader, I stepped onto a large block. Then I held out my hand to assist Judy.

"Come on, Connie," she said.

When Blanca stepped onto the ice, it dipped, and she slid feetfirst into the icy water. The second time she tried, the ice dipped again.

"Why don't you get on another block?" I said.

"I'm scared! Let Alice try," Blanca said.

When Alice stepped onto the ice, it started to sink. She backed off. I jumped toward the bank with Judy and Connie on my heels. Blanca began to cry, because water had gotten inside her rubbers.

"My feet are cold, and I am wet. I want to go back," she cried.

I looked out into the river and realized what a bad idea that had been. We never would have gotten anywhere. We might have even drowned. For a short time, my great adventure came to a standstill.

Blanca kept crying, "I want to go back. Someone has to go with me."

"We planned this for weeks. I don't want to go back," said Alice.

Connie and Judy chimed in, "We don't want to go back, either."

Blanca was crying uncontrollably and shivering. Her leggings were soaked as wet as her feet.

I was upset and angry because this was something I had wanted to do for a long time. All I could think about was that my adventure was just beginning and could so quickly end.

"I am not going back!" I shouted.

When Alice realized that no one else would return with Blanca, she shuffled around in the snow for a few minutes in disappointment and then said, "OK, I'll go back with her."

"Promise you won't tell anybody where we are," I said.

"I promise," Blanca whimpered.

"Me too," said Alice.

They walked toward the direction of the path leading back up the mountain. I knew we would be far away by the time they got back to Sacred Heart.

Still determined to have my great adventure, I did not want to show any signs of fear because I was their so-called leader. In the stories I had told, the leader was always brave and fearless. "Follow me," I said to Judy and Connie.

"Where are we going?" asked Judy.

"We're going to follow the railroad tracks," I answered.

I had no idea where the tracks would lead us or what we would do once we got there. It was already dark outside, but the moon's glow lighting the pristine snow helped. The darker it became, the more frightened we were, but I was determined not to show any signs of fear because I was their so-called leader. In the stories I had told, the leader was always brave and fearless. The crunching of the snow under our feet seemed to magnify with every step. Our rubbers and heavy clothing made it difficult to maintain a steady pace. We walked for a short time, and then, since there was no place we could sit, we stood in place to rest. I listened for a train but could hear no sounds.

"I'm tired. The snow is too deep," complained Connie.

"Well, when a train comes by, we should hop on it," I said.

What was I thinking? Hopping a train was possible in one of my stories but not in the reality of that night. I, the leader, would have had to jump onto the train first. At that moment I no longer wanted to be the leader of this adventure. Needless to say, had a train approached and we tried such an outrageous feat, we could have been killed.

We had no idea how long we had been walking.

"Let's rest," said Judy.

"No, we'll freeze to death out here. We have to keep walking," I said.

Judy and Connie were the best friends to have with me on that journey. If they had not been with me, I don't know what would have happened to me. If they had known how frightened I was, they would have insisted we go back. We were chilled and afraid, but we kept following the train tracks. Eventually we saw a huge bridge quite a distance from us. In my mind, the bridge became our destination. There were houses sparsely located up on the hills but not in our immediate vicinity.

"I'm cold and tired," Connie said.

"I am hungry. I can't go any farther unless we stop and eat something," Judy said.

I had forgotten about our snacks. We stopped to take out our food.

"Let's eat while we walk," I suggested. As we walked, I turned back, happy to see our progress in a trail of footprints. The cookies took our minds off the walk, but not for long.

"What if a bear or wolf comes after us?" Connie asked. "Let's go back! I'm scared!"

"Connie, there are no wolves or bears around here," I explained, "Where did you get that idea?"

"In one of the stories you told us...."

I interrupted her thought. "Connie, this is not a story. This is real. Come on, let's just keep walking," I said.

As we walked, the bridge in the distance seemed larger, and I got more excited. After walking for some time, Judy stopped and said, "I'm tired. Are you sure you don't want to turn back?"

"We can't go back now. We've come too far. It's going to take us a long time to get back," I said.

We were tired and cold, and there was no sign of shelter. I did not want to hear any more talk about turning back. If they had known how frightened I was, we already would have been on our way back. The farther we walked, the more convinced I became that it was time to turn around, but I did not want to tell them. I decided that if one of them complained again, we would turn back. As we continued to walk, I made up a story about an exciting adventure to keep our minds off of the cold. Neither of them complained for a while—although I was beginning to wish they would. The full moon lit our path through sparkling deep snow, which had crept inside our rubbers and shoes. My feet felt as if they were frozen, making it harder and harder for me to walk. Judy and Connie had to feel the same. I didn't know how much farther we could walk. I was ready to turn back but did not want to suggest it.

Judy asked, "How much farther do we have to go?"

That bridge was still too far away, so I said, "We'll climb up the hill to the next house we see."

We did see tiny lights up in the hills, but they also were too far away. We walked and walked and walked. Connie began to cry.

"We'll see a house soon," I promised as we trudged on.

I do not know how long we walked before we spotted what we thought was a house up in the hills; it looked like a speck in the faraway distance.

"I see lights up there. It must be a house!" shouted Judy. "We can climb up to that one."

We were excited. Judy was the first to start the climb, and we followed. The lights were so far away, but that did not stop us. More snow got into our rubbers. Our mittens got wet as we grabbed onto bushes and whatever else was there as we pulled and dug our way upward. It was dark now, because the trees blocked so much of the moonlight—making this the scariest part of the journey. *Maybe Connie was right—maybe there were bears or wolves in these hills,* I thought. If they attacked and ate us, no one would ever know. The nuns would not even know where to look for us. Connie fell and slid a few times.

"Hold my hand," Judy told her.

I took Connie's other hand, but as it was hard to climb that way, I let go, leaving Judy to lead the way. *The real leader does not always have to be in front,* I thought. Every time one of us slid or fell, we stopped to rest. We were on our way out of that wilderness. It seemed to take hours to finally reach the house, but it probably took the same amount of time it would have taken us to return to the home.

We finally reached our destination. Close up, the house was huge. We stood behind it and looked at each other. None of us wanted to knock on the door. Judy and Connie simultaneously looked at me, and I knew what that meant. We walked to the back door of the house, and I knocked. No one came to the door, so I knocked harder a second time. An elderly white woman opened the door.

"Miss, we are from Sacred Heart Home, and we are lost," I said.

She invited us into her home and told us to sit at the kitchen table. She offered us cocoa and cookies, which we were glad to accept. The warmth of the cup held within our cold hands felt so good. I gulped mine down while Judy and Connie were still sipping from their cups. The cocoa warmed my entire body. I wanted more but was afraid to ask for another cup.

The woman made a telephone call as we drank the cocoa and ate our cookies. We did not know who she had called until a policeman appeared.

"Are you the girls from Sacred Heart?" one asked.

Connie dropped her cup into its saucer. We replied in unison by shaking our heads in the affirmative.

"Do you know there have been a lot of people out looking for you girls? How did you get this far?" the other policeman asked.

We were too afraid to answer. They were amazed at the distance we had walked in that weather. "Finish your cocoa, and then you are coming with us," they said.

I wondered where they were planning to take us. Would they take us to jail because we had run away? That is where they would have taken us in one of my stories.

When we were settled in the police car, we discovered they would be taking us back to Sacred Heart. I was relieved to hear that. Connie cried and sniffled during the entire ride back, but Judy and I remained silent. During that ride, my thoughts were about what would happen to us when we got back to the home. I thought about the type of punishment we might receive for what we had done. Our punishment would probably be worse than any ever given before. No one else had ever run away and been brought back by the police.

When the car stopped, we all walked up the steps to the big doors. Mother Superior, who was the head of all the nuns, greeted us with a look on her face I had never seen before. She spoke with the two men, but we could not hear what was said.

"Follow me," Mother Superior said.

As we passed other nuns on our way to Mother Superior's office, the other nuns smiled and nodded their heads at us. I was surprised at their reaction, because they were always impersonal and avoided any show of affection. I nudged Judy with my elbow.

"Wow, they are glad to see us," I whispered.

"Be quiet, and follow me," Mother Superior demanded.

I thought, *She has good ears.*

We entered her dimly lit office, and she sat behind the big, wooden desk. "Take off your coat and rubbers," she said.

I slowly unbuttoned my coat, laid it across the back of a chair, and nervously tugged at one rubber while standing, but I could not pull it off. Pulling and pulling, I was unable to get the rubber off, so I sat on the floor, which made that task much easier. Water dripped from the rubber onto the hardwood floor. Pulling off the other was less troublesome. My shoes and socks were wet and my feet cold. Mother Superior stared at us through her wire-rimmed glasses. She did not allow us to remove our wet shoes and socks—which I considered punishment.

We stood in stunned silence and waited for permission to sit down.

"Sit down," she finally ordered. Then she asked, "Where did you think you were going?"

When Connie heard that, her cries and sniffles got louder. She sobbed so hard that it looked as if she were gasping for breath. She had not stopped crying since we had left the woman's house. Judy and I held our heads down, afraid to look into Mother Superior's cold eyes and stern face. Neither of us answered her question. We remained silent. Our reply would not have been good enough.

"Did you think you would not be found?"

No one uttered a word.

"You could have been hurt out there. Did you think about that?"

Neither of us answered, but Connie's sobs continued to get louder with every word from Mother Superior.

"Were Alice and Blanca with you?"

I had not thought about them until that moment. Alice and Blanca must have kept our secret, so I shook my head from side to side and looked at Judy. She did the same.

"They were missing for a long time and told me they had been playing behind the dormitory and were locked outside," said Mother Superior.

What a relief it was to know they had made it back safely.

Mother Superior did not raise her voice. "From now on, you cannot go outside without my permission. You will remain inside doing chores or in the playroom while the others are outside. And you will not get any dessert for one month. If you receive visitors, whatever you are given will be taken away."

That was something I did not have to worry about.

"Now get your things together, and follow me," Mother Superior ordered.

She took us upstairs to one of the bedrooms over the medical offices and gave us each a nightgown. I did not know what time it was, but it must have been very late. Mother Superior never asked us if we had eaten anything, so I guess putting us to bed without eating was another punishment. I was surprised that we did not get paddled. We were paddled for behavior less serious than what we had done. What we had done was very serious.

Although none of the nuns ever told us so, I believe our running away frightened them more than it did us. After what I considered an exciting adventure, I knew that the next time I ran away would only be in my stories. I now had a lot of new and real material.

CHAPTER SIX

# A CHANGE OF VENUE

Mass was required for everyone unless we were sick. The morning after our adventure, we sat in the church balcony separated from the other girls. After church, we were taken to our dining room to join the others. Everyone was happy and excited to see us. My eyes scanned the room for Alice and Blanca. I noticed Alice first, and as our eyes met we both smiled. But when Blanca and I made eye contact, she looked away. Mother Augustina came into our dining room and we all lowered our heads. It was time to recite our prayer before eating.

"Bless us, oh, Lord, and these thy gifts, which we are about to receive from thy bounty through Christ our Lord, Amen."

I prayed without giving thought to what I was saying. (Now when I pray before eating a meal, however, I truly know what I am saying and why. Most importantly I choose to do it.) We were not allowed to talk while we ate, but each of the girls at my table had asked me a question before I could answer any one of them. There had always been rumors and whispers of girls wanting to run away but, prior to that time, no one actually had. Our adventure was unique, so everyone was interested and wanted to know every detail of our journey.

Our punishment of being kept inside during play lasted for weeks, so we were glad when bad weather prevented the other girls from going outside. At least during those times, we had the chance to play with others and were able to sit down and tell our adventure to more girls at one time.

Everything seemed to go on as usual for several months until one afternoon, while in the playroom, Sister Augustina said to me, "Jo-Ann, Mother Superior wants you in her office right now!"

"Ooh, you're in trouble," some of the girls said.

I was surprised, because being sent to Mother Superior's office was unusual. None of us was ever told to go to her office unless it was for something very important. I had not been in trouble since the runaway.

*What does she want with me?* I wondered. It was a big deal to be summoned. Most girls hurried to get there, but that day I stopped and spoke with everyone I met on the way. And when being told where I was going, they were surprised I had stopped to talk.

When I arrived at the office, there was a thin, black woman sitting in one of the chairs. "This is Miss Johnson," Mother Superior said. "Say hello to Miss Johnson."

"Hello, Miss Johnson," I said as commanded.

Immediately after my reply, Mother Superior said, "You are going to live with Miss Johnson."

I was so shocked. I was speechless. I wanted her to tell me why I was going to live with this stranger. No one ever questioned Mother Superior, but I needed to do so that day. Miss Johnson smiled at me, but I was unable to return the gesture. My mind was racing. *Where is my mother? Why isn't she here to get me? Why am I going to live with a stranger? Maybe the nuns think I am going to run away again. They don't want me, the ring leader, to influence the other girls. This probably is the best way to keep me from them.*

Mother Superior must have begun to work on this plan immediately after I had run away. Maybe my mother was dead or they could not get in touch with her or she did not want me anymore. Why? Years later, as an adult, I learned that I had lived under the supervision of the Poughkeepsie Department of Welfare all those years.

I was not given a chance to say good-bye to my friends or to pack anything to take with me. This was the cruelest punishment of all. To my surprise, Mother Superior gave Miss Johnson a box containing clothes for me.

The ride to my new home was quiet. Miss Johnson sat in the front seat of the car with the driver, and I sat in the back. Big, beautiful houses lined both sides of the street. I had never seen streets or houses like that before. We stopped in front of a large, white house with a porch. I followed Miss Johnson inside. She took me into a room where an elderly, robust woman sat.

"Mother, this is Jo-Ann," she said.

Her mother smiled and in a soft voice said, "Hello, child." Her smile and tone of voice already made me feel welcome. I immediately liked her.

"Jo-Ann, this is my mother, Mrs. Johnson," said Miss Johnson.

I politely replied, "Hello, Mrs. Johnson."

"Mary Jane will show you around the house and to your room," Mrs. Johnson said.

My ears perked up when I learned I would have my own room.

My new home address was 69 Liberty Street, in Kingston, New York, which was located approximately ten or twelve miles from Sacred Heart Orphan Asylum. I was excited to live in my first home and have my own bedroom. I did not remember ever having a home with my mother.

Mrs. Johnson's husband, George, was deceased. She had two adult children, neither of whom was married. Her daughter, Mary Jane, was a tall, lanky woman who was probably in her mid-to-late twenties. Her son, Peter, was a tall, stocky man probably in his thirties. Mary Jane worked in a factory, and Peter was a truck driver who was away from home a great deal of time. Mrs. Johnson was known by her husband's name, Mrs. George Johnson. She was always called Mrs. Johnson. I was never told her first name. Mrs. Johnson was a short, dark-skinned, robust woman with large breasts that met her waist, and she had big hips. She may have been in her sixties.

Their house was big. The only other house that I had ever been in was the home of the white woman who had taken us in when I had run away from Sacred Heart. I remembered sitting at her kitchen table but nothing else about the house. Mary Jane and I walked to the front door. To the right was a room with a large black piano, which I later learned was a baby grand. Other rooms downstairs were a living room with a television, couch, and some chairs, a bathroom, two bedrooms, and a kitchen. The laundry room with its washing machine was next to the kitchen. There were three bedrooms and an attic upstairs. The tour ended at the room that was to be mine.

Mary Jane pointed to a piece of furniture with a mirror on top and said, "This dresser is for your clothes."

At the time I had nothing of my own to put in it, only the few things in the box given to me by Mother Superior. I felt good knowing that the dresser was mine. The bed was against the wall with a window above it. Later that day when I was alone in my bedroom, I stood on the bed and looked out of the window into a large backyard. Wow! I had my very own bedroom and a place to call home. If this was my punishment for running away from Sacred Heart, perhaps I should have run away sooner.

Mrs. Johnson and Mary Jane played the piano. I learned that Mrs. Johnson had previously given piano lessons but no longer did so. Her current occupation was washing and ironing clothes for other families, all of whom were white. Sometimes I would sit at the kitchen table and watch her put clothes into the washing machine. Then I would follow her to the backyard and pass her clothespins as she hung them on the line. The crisp, white shirts and linen filled one side of the backyard. Mrs. Johnson starched and ironed the shirts. Her ironing board stood in the kitchen, where we talked as I often sat and watched her iron. She ironed and folded each shirt and piece of linen before placing it into a large basket.

Most of Mrs. Johnson's day was spent in the kitchen, because when she was not washing or ironing, she was cooking. I believe the kitchen was her favorite room in the house. Everything Mrs. Johnson cooked was delicious. Prior to living with them, I had never seen a meal prepared. There was a large television in the living room, but I never saw her sit down to watch it. Much of my time also was spent in the kitchen or in the living room watching television.

Every Sunday morning Mary Jane and I would walk several miles from the house to attend mass at St. Joseph's Church. Mrs. Johnson never went to church with us, and Mary Jane did not drive. I often wondered if my attending church every week was part an agreement made between the Johnson family and Sacred Heart before I could live with them.

PS 8 was located on Franklin Street, which was a block from our house and was the first public school I would attend. I could look out one of the living room windows and see part of the school playground. The biggest surprise on my first day of school was that I found myself in the awkward position of being a new student in a school where both girls and boys attended. Another surprise was that we did not have assembly every morning. Catechism was not a subject taught, nor was poetry. Because catechism was not taught at the school, the Catholic students were let out of school early every Wednesday to attend catechism class at St. Joseph's School near the church. We enjoyed our walks there. Sometimes we stopped at a store, and those with money would buy cookies or candy. We laughed, joked, and sometimes raced to the school.

The class sizes at the public school were much larger than those I was used to at the parochial school. Compared to Sacred Heart, the courses at PS 8 were easy, because I had already been taught most of it. I was soon bored and restless in those classrooms and resumed some of my mischievous, attention-getting ways. I remember the time I got into trouble for rubber-band shooting a bobby pin at the teacher whose back was to the class as she wrote on the blackboard. Another incident occurred when I got into a loud shouting match with a boy who sat behind me, but I do not remember why we were yelling.

During Christmas season at PS 8, we made Christmas-tree ornaments in art class. Some were made with lightbulbs we brought from home. One of the girls in my class made what I thought was the prettiest ornament with different colors of glitter. That ornament would have looked nice on any Christmas tree. When students left the art class, I sneaked back inside the room and put that ornament inside my coat pocket. While on my way home from school, I removed the ornament from my pocket, and it dropped and broke. I was almost in tears.

At the time, the fact that I had stolen something did not seem to bother me. At Sacred Heart, we had always been taught that stealing was a sin, and if we had stolen anything and were caught, we would have been punished. Before that time, I had never stolen anything. I told myself that my punishment for having stolen the ornament was the fact that it broke. I do not remember the name of the girl to whom the ornament belonged, but the next day at school while walking upstairs to the second floor, she asked, "Jo-Ann, have you seen my Christmas ornament?"

I rushed passed her, not wanting to say a word, but I guess my conscience bothered me. I turned back toward her and replied, "No. I have not seen it," and kept walking. Nevertheless, whenever I was in her presence, I felt guilty because I had committed two sins: I stole, and I lied.

When I first attended public school, I did not have any friends. Mrs. Johnson gave me a chore so that I could earn money. That chore was to deliver the basket of ironed clothes to the home of Mrs. Steinberg, who lived about four blocks from Mrs. Johnson. I was paid ten cents or sometimes twenty cents by Mrs. Steinberg upon delivery. She was a nice lady who sometimes offered me a glass of Tang, which I always accepted. The opportunity to receive money for delivering clothes was a big deal to me. Before living with the Johnsons, I had never even handled money, and now I was able to work for my own money.

My introduction to the outside world was through the Johnson family. The time I spent with them was an interesting and important learning experience. I was, and always will be, grateful that they provided a house that was a home. Prior to living with the Johnsons, I had never had the freedom to walk to a store or to listen to the radio and watch television daily if I wanted. Though I was a young girl at the time, I unknowingly soaked in as much as I possibly could. I did not want to ever forget anything about my life with the Johnsons. Learning to play the piano was fun, although there were times I would have preferred to be outside playing with my friends. We were never allowed to touch a piano at Sacred Heart, and piano lessons were unthinkable. It did not take long for me to get used to waking up every morning, eating breakfast, and going to school without having to attend church first. It was new and exciting for me.

My whole experience with the Johnsons was as if I were living a dream. On school days, after eating dinner and doing my homework, I was allowed to watch television. We did have a television room at Sacred Heart next to the dormitory, but the only television programs we were allowed to watch were *Bishop J. Sheen*, wherein the bishop talked about religion, and sometimes Roy Rogers, the cowboy. I ate a variety of new foods at the Johnsons. Cornflakes, chicken, chicken feet, eel, and many other foods I had not heard of were introduced to me.

Before moving in with the Johnsons, I had never listened to a radio. The first time I listened to a radio was at my new best friends Joan and Lillie's house, and I especially enjoyed rock 'n' roll. One Saturday afternoon Mary Jane took me to my first dance. There I learned to do the stroll, which was the popular dance at that time. Learning that dance was fun and easy, because I felt as if I had done it before. It reminded me of shinning floors at Sacred Heart. We made shining those floors an exciting and enjoyable chore. I danced and smiled all the time, thinking about how shiny the dance floor would be with a rag under my foot.

Most of my memories of living with the Johnsons were positive ones, but my favorite was of having my own bedroom with windows I could look out of and a dresser to put my clothes into. At night I lay in bed and heard only silence—no girls crying, coughing, or snoring. In my mind, I recounted what I had done that day and planned for the following day. Those good thoughts ushered me into a good night's sleep. Sometimes I would retreat to my room, lie across my bed, and think about what the girls at Sacred Heart would be doing at that particular moment.

Other times I looked out of the windows into the backyard to watch the crisp clothes hanging from the clotheslines blow in the breeze. Seeing those clothes blowing in all directions made me feel happy. The clothespins were the only restraints that prevented the clothes from flying away. While at Sacred Heart, I considered my restraints to be the nuns and rules, religion and church, buildings and stone walls. But the fact that at the Johnsons, I was allowed to look out of a window for any length of time I wanted gave me a sense of freedom. At Sacred Heart, when we looked out of the dormitory front windows, we saw the playground. The back windows overlooked the Hudson River, where there always seemed to be large boats or barges moving slowly. My restraints at the Johnson home were minor. It felt so good knowing that I was free to go outside into the backyard to play whenever I wanted. When playing outside, I was as free as a bird in flight.

## CHAPTER SEVEN

# NEW BEST FRIENDS

One morning while mingling on the playground before school, two girls walked up to me. "Hi, what's your name?" the taller of the two asked.

Before I could answer, she said, "My name is Joan."

"I'm Lillie. We're sisters," the other girl said.

"Are you new at this school? I haven't seen you here before," Joan said.

"I am new here. My name is Jo-Ann."

"Where do you live?" asked Lillie.

"I live on Liberty Street, across from the school."

"Do you want to play after school?" Joan asked.

"Sure, but I have to get permission from Mrs. Johnson first," I replied.

"Who's Mrs. Johnson?"

Before I could answer, the bell rang, and it was time to go inside.

When I arrived home from school that afternoon, I went directly to the kitchen where Mrs. Johnson was ironing and said to her, "I met two girls at school today, and they asked me to play with them on the playground. Tomorrow after school can I play with them?"

"What are their names?"

"They are sisters. One is Joan, and the other is Lillie."

"What is their last name?"

"I don't know. I didn't ask, but they are very friendly."

"Do you know where they live?" she asked.

"No."

"Jo-Ann, I want to meet them first. After school tomorrow, bring them home with you so that I can meet them."

"OK," I replied.

I was so excited. I could barely wait until the next morning so that I could tell them.

Joan was the older of the two. They both had thick, long, black hair worn in ponytails. The next morning as soon as I arrived on the school grounds, I began looking for them. When I saw them, I was happy and excited.

I said to them, "Mrs. Johnson said I could play with you after school, but she wants to meet you first. Can you go home with me after school so that she can meet you?"

"Who is Mrs. Johnson?" Judy asked.

"She is the lady I live with."

"She is not your mother?" Lillie asked.

"No. I used to live at a girls' home, and now I live with Mrs. Johnson and her daughter, Mary Jane. I'll show you my house. You can see if from the other side of the school yard."

We walked to the opposite side of the school, and I pointed to the house.

"Wow! That's a big house," exclaimed Lillie. Although it was the smallest house on the block, It was big to us.

"After school, let's meet by the back door," I suggested.

"OK," Joan agreed.

We met after school, and they walked home with me. I took them to the living room to sit down while I went into the kitchen.

"Mrs. Johnson, Joan and Lillie are here," I said.

"Tell them to come in here, child," Mrs. Johnson said.

I brought them in for introductions.

"This is Mrs. Johnson," I said.

"Hi. I'm Joan."

"I'm Lillie."

"What is your mother and father's name?" Mrs. Johnson asked.

"We live with our father. His name is Frank Wilson," Joan said.

"Where do you live?"

"We live on Van Buren Street," Lillie replied.

Mrs. Johnson looked them over from head to toe. "Jo-Ann can play with you on the school grounds, but she cannot leave and go anyplace else. Come home before dinner, Jo-Ann."

"OK," I agreed. We usually ate dinner around the same time every evening, which was after Mary Jane arrived home from work.

"You can go play now," said Mrs. Johnson.

"Thank you, Mrs. Johnson," I replied.

"Good-bye," Joan and Lillie said.

We ran back to the school yard to play tag. We played tag for a while and then sat on the school steps and watched some of the other kids. That was the most fun I had had since I had moved there.

One Saturday afternoon Joan and Lillie came to my house to ask Mrs. Johnson if I could go out and play. She agreed, and as we walked toward the school playground, Joan said, "Let's go to our house."

Without hesitating, I replied, "OK."

Their house was about five blocks from mine. I followed them home to discover a very small, yellow, wooden house trimmed in green. As soon as I entered their home, I realized how fortunate I was. The Johnsons' house was the only one I could compare to their home. When the front door was opened, the short hallway was lit momentarily. There was a door to the right, which led to a small bathroom with a toilet and sink. The main door opened into the kitchen where there were a large wood stove, a sink, and some metal cabinets. Their living room, to the left of the kitchen, contained a big couch and a chair. The only light into the living room was the light from the kitchen when the curtain was pulled aside. There was a radio on a small, wooden table. Another curtain separated the kitchen from their bedroom, in which were a dresser and large bed that they shared. Clothes were piled on top of the dresser, and the drawers overflowed with clothes. The bedroom separated from their room with a curtain belonged to their father. Joan and Lillie were always clean and neat with their thick hair neatly pulled back into a braided ponytail. They never spoke about their mother.

We went into the living room. Lillie plopped onto the chair, and Joan and I sat on the couch. We were talking when we heard the kitchen door open.

"Hi, Daddy," they said in unison.

"Hey," he said as he walked into the living room.

"Daddy, this is our friend, Jo-Ann," Joan said.

"Hello, Mr. Wilson," I said.

"Hey, there," he replied. Their father was a tall, dark man with thick eyebrows who walked slowly and looked tired. He put wood inside the stove as we continued to talk.

They came home with me a couple of times before I was told that they were no longer allowed to come back and I was forbidden to return to their home. When I asked the reason, I was told it was because there was no adult at the house, and their mother did not live with them. Their father was always at work and did not come home until evening. Joan and Lillie were my only friends. Whom would I play with? How unfair!

I disobeyed, however, and continued my friendship with Joan and Lillie. Sometimes we actually played on the school grounds, but other times I met them on one of the corners of the school property and went to their home.

One Saturday afternoon I again disobeyed Mrs. Johnson and went to Joan and Lillie's home. When I got home, she asked where I had been. I did not immediately answer her.

"Jo-Ann, I asked where you have been?" Mrs. Johnson never raised her voice, but the stern look on her face was enough to make me answer.

"I was playing on the school grounds with Joan and Lillie."

The disappointment in her voice was apparent when she said, "Jo-Ann, tell me the truth."

Almost in a whisper with my voice quivering, I responded, "I was playing at Joan and Lillie's house." With Mrs. Johnson, more than any adult I had ever met, I felt uneasy admitting my disobedience.

That day I found out that Mrs. Johnson had a friend named Mrs. Burns who lived on the same street as Joan and Lillie. She had told Mrs. Johnson that she saw me there. Mrs. Johnson was very disappointed that I had been lying to her and continued to go to my friends' home. She told me that the only place I was allowed to play for the next two weeks was in the backyard. My punishment seemed to last much longer. Although I could play in our backyard, Joan and Lillie were not allowed to come over to play with me. There was not much playing to do by myself, so I would read. When I was inside the house, Mrs. Johnson would let me watch television. Sometimes I went into the attic and rummaged through old boxes and records. There were quite a few record piles that I looked through, and I realized someone in the Johnson household liked Fats Domino. There were more of his records than any others.

When my two weeks of punishment were finally over, I did not know what to do. Should I ask to go to the school grounds and play, or should I pretend that the day had not come? Mrs. Johnson had been so good to me that I did not want to do anything else to disappoint her. Unlike the nuns, she never raised her voice at me or hit me over the head with a dust mop, pinched my ears, or paddled me. Her words and actions let me know she cared about me. I spent more time with Mrs. Johnson than with Mary Jane, and at times I wished she were my mother.

I wanted to play with Joan and Lillie at the playground or any place else, but I did not ask. Joan and Lillie were my friends. I missed them so much. It was a week after my punishment ended, and I was helping Mrs. Johnson remove clothes from the line. She surprised me when she said, "Jo-Ann, aren't you going to ask if you can play on the playground anymore?"

Startled, I dropped the bag of clothespins. I did not know how to respond. Finally I said, "I wanted to but was afraid to ask you."

"I don't mind you playing on the school playground, but that is as far as you can go."

I placed the clothespin bag inside the clothes basket and wrapped my arms around her waist. "Thank you, Mrs. Johnson," I said.

"OK, child, let's get back to work."

The next day I did go to the school playground and looked for Joan and Lillie, but they were not there. I spent some time on the playground but not as much as I would have if my friends were there. The Johnsons had a telephone. Even if I could have used it, the only calls I would have made would have been to Joan and Lillie, and they did not have a telephone in their house. I missed seeing and talking with them. They were the only playmates I had when not in school. They did not know my punishment was over, and there was only one way for me to let them know, so I went to their house.

I knocked on the door and saw Lillie's face pressed against the living-room window. She motioned me in with her hand. When I stepped inside the small, dark hallway, I rushed to open the other door for light. I do not remember seeing a light fixture in the ceiling but do not remember looking for one, either. If they had one, maybe the lightbulb had burned out, or they only turned it on at night. Although the hallway was short, I would not have wanted to walk through it at night.

"Hi." Although I was off my punishment, I hoped Mrs. Johnson's friend did not see me. I sarcastically remarked, "I walked over from the next block and ran across the street to get here. I hope Miss Nosey Body didn't see me!"

"Come on and sit down. We're listening to the radio," Joan said.

"What are you listening to?"

"There was just a song on by Elvis Presley."

"Who is Elvis Presley?"

They looked at each other and laughed. Joan said, "Don't you know who Elvis Presley is?"

"No."

"Everybody likes Elvis Presley. He is a white guy who sings good music."

Lillie said, "Yeah, but I heard he said that all black people can do for him is play his music and shine his shoes."

"If he said that, why are you listening to his music?" I asked.

"This station comes in better than the others. They play a lot of his music," said Lillie.

"OK," I said.

"I missed you," I said cheerfully. "I wasn't allowed to leave the house—not even to go to the store. If Mrs. Johnson had let me to go to the store, I would have sneaked over here to see you."

Lillie leaned back as if swallowed by her chair. "Yeah, and if Mrs. Johnson found out, she probably would have punished you for two months."

"Yeah, you are right," I said.

"What did you do during your punishment?" Joan asked.

"I just read, watched television, and helped Mrs. Johnson around the house."

"Do you like to read?"

"I love to read, because I can travel to different places, experience different adventures, and learn about other people."

"What did you read while you were being punished?" Lillie asked.

"I read *The Three Musketeers*."

"What kind of book is *The Three Musketeers*?" Lillie asked as she sat twirling her finger around her ponytail.

Joan asked, "Isn't that a book for boys?"

"No. Books are for anybody who wants to read them," I replied.

Joan was sitting next to me on the sofa doing the same thing with her ponytail that her sister was doing. "Jo-Ann, do you have a lot of books?" she asked. "I have a few," I responded.

"Will you let us read some of your books? The only books we have are schoolbooks." Joan said.

I did not immediately respond, because I felt very sad when I heard her say that. It meant when they were not in school, they played with each other or listened to the radio. Their home was very small and dark, so they really did not have a lot of room to run around and play. I guess most of their playing was done outside when the weather permitted. Their father probably prepared their dinner when he returned home from work.

"Sure," I said. "The next time I come over, I will bring a couple of books with me. I'd better leave now. Do you want to walk back to the playground with me?"

"OK," they replied.

The next time I returned to their home, I took some books. They were just as happy to receive them as I was to share the books with them. I knew those books would take them away from their little, yellow house into an entirely different world.

I learned friendship and kindness from Joan and Lillie. They always offered to share what little they had. Being able to share a saltine cracker with them meant more to me than eating a meal at the Johnsons. Eating three meals a day at the Johnsons was normal, but I do not know if that was the case at Joan and Lillie's house. I believe they really could not afford to share their food; however, they offered me a cracker. Their offer was a sacrifice made from the heart with the purest intentions. I believe I did what a good friend would do. I accepted their offer and enjoyed eating that delicious cracker with my friends. Sometimes the little things we do in life are the most meaningful. They taught me this life lesson, for which I am grateful.

My friends in Kingston taught me that a child does not have to live in a large, beautiful house filled with lavish furnishings and a refrigerator filled with food to be happy. The love and nourishment within the home are the most important components in a truly happy dwelling. I had never been in a home with such meager furnishings but an abundance of love. My friends never complained about their situation or the material things they lacked. Their constant smiles left an indelible, positive impression.

CHAPTER EIGHT

# NEW PATHWAYS

I continued to disobey Mrs. Johnson and sneak to Joan and Lillie's house. One afternoon while they were walking me back toward the school, we were chased by a large, red, long-haired dog. That was the first time I remember seeing a dog. It was so big. We ran and scattered in different directions, with me running onto someone's porch. The dog followed me onto the porch, and I tried to jump over the banister to get away—and fell. When I got up, I could not stand on my left foot. Something was terribly wrong. Joan and Lillie tried to help me, but I was unable to walk. So they knocked on the door of the home and explained what had happened. I don't recall much after that incident, but I later found out that I had a broken leg.

My classmates learned of my broken leg when I did not return to school, and some of them came to my house to see me. They signed my cast—which really surprised me. When not in school, the only kids I hung out with were Joan and Lillie, but my cast was full of signatures. The teachers allowed my schoolwork to be sent home so that I would not fall behind in my studies. I lived only a block from the school, so getting my homework and sending it back was not a problem.

Soon I became bored sitting at home all day, every day, so I asked Mrs. Johnson if she would teach me to play the piano.

She replied, "Not unless you are sure you really want to do this."

"I'm sure. I want to learn how to play the piano."

"I'll teach you, but it will take a lot of your time. You must be willing to practice every day."

"I will," I said cheerfully.

"All right. Go sit at the piano, and I will be there in a little while."

I lifted the piano cover and fiddled with the piano keys for a few minutes before Mrs. Johnson came into the room.

"Are you sure you want to learn to play the piano?"

"Yes, Mrs. Johnson. Yes!"

"This means you will have to practice every day. Even when your leg gets better, piano lessons will come before going out to play. There may be days you will not go outside to play. Do you understand?"

"Yes."

"Do you still want to learn?"

Without hesitation I replied, "Yes!"

"Stand up." Mrs. Johnson lifted the top of the piano seat and pulled out a music book. Mrs. Johnson's hands were big, but when her fingers glided over those piano keys, the music was mesmerizing. I watched her fingers and listened to the music and wondered if I would ever play the piano like that. Sister Christina's music never sounded like this.

"Mrs. Johnson, I have never heard music played like this before. It's beautiful," I said.

"One day you'll be able to play this way if you practice hard," she said.

My first lesson was to learn to play the scales and chords with my right hand. I had to replay them over and over. The next thing I learned was to play them with my left hand, and after that, I learned to play them with both hands at the same time. In other sessions, she taught me how to read music lines, spaces, and notes. Whenever I was not doing school work or reading, I would practice playing the piano.

During that time, what shocked me most was that Mrs. Johnson or Mary Jane never scolded or punished me for being on Van Buren Street the day I broke my leg. I do not remember ever being asked what I had been doing in that area or whom I had been with at the time. They probably already knew.

The day finally came for my cast to be removed. On that day, the doctor took some type of saw to remove the cast, and when it was removed, my left leg looked like a thin, ashy stick with peeling skin. When we got home, Mrs. Johnson gave me Vaseline to rub on my leg daily. I wore long socks to cover my ugly leg and hoped that the sock made it look larger.

## CHAPTER NINE

# CURIOSITY

On my first day back to school, while on the school grounds, I noticed a boy walk past. I had never seen him at our school, so he must have been on his way to another one. He was cute, thin, well dressed and wore a cap. I watched him until he was no longer in sight. I was eleven years old the first time I had noticed a boy with interest. Every day after that day, I managed to be at that same area on the school grounds and at the same time so that I could see him walk by.

When I returned home from school that day, I rushed into the kitchen, sat at the table, and hurriedly did my homework. On that day, I did not stop to chat with Mrs. Johnson as I normally did while doing homework.

When I was done, I said, "Mrs. Johnson, can I go outside now?"

"Don't you remember our agreement? You have piano lessons," she said.

"Can I go out after I practice?" I asked as I hurried to the piano room.

Without answering, she came into the piano room and sat down beside me. Each practice session started with my having to play the scales and chords several times. She watched and listened. I continued until she placed a sheet of music in front of me and told me to play it. My mind was not on the music, which was evident during my practice.

With a stern voice, Mrs. Johnson said, "Jo-Ann, lift your wrists. Read the notes. Concentrate."

I was unable to concentrate on the music notes or piano keys because my mind was on going to my friends' house. No matter how hard, I tried the music was awful.

"What's wrong with you today, Jo-Ann? Maybe you have not been practicing enough."

My ears perked up when I heard her say that, because practicing an hour a day seemed more than enough time to me.

"This music is hard. Can you give me something easier to practice?" I asked.

"No. Today this is what I want you to practice. Take your time."

During the times I had practiced when my leg was in a cast, that hour seemed much shorter. However, on this particular day, the hour seemed so much longer. By the time I finished practicing, it was too late to go outside.

I continued this routine for several weeks before I confronted Mrs. Johnson and said, "Mrs. Johnson, I don't want to play the piano anymore."

"Why?"

"I want to go outside and play with the other kids."

"Do you remember what I told you when you first asked me to teach you to play the piano? I told you that your piano lessons would come first. And that's what I mean."

With a frown on my face, I replied, "Yes, but I don't want to learn to play the piano if I can't go outside and play anymore."

"You'll be able to go outside on Saturday, but during the week, you will stay in and practice. That's all there is to it," she said.

"But all the other kids can go out to play after school."

"You are not the other kids, and you will do what I say." That was the first time I heard disappointment in Mrs. Johnson's voice and saw it in her face. She spoke louder than normal and had a serious look on her face. I could hardly wait until Saturday, but when that day arrived and I was allowed out, I headed straight for Joan and Lillie's house. When I arrived, they were sitting on the front porch, and I was just in time to catch a glimpse of that cute boy walk up the steps and into the house across the street.

"Who is he?" I asked.

"Oh, that's Sheldon Brown. He lives over there with his mother," Joan replied.

I said, "Some mornings when I'm on the school grounds, I see him walk past our school."

"He goes to a different school."

"Does he have any sisters or brothers?" I asked.

"No."

"The next time you're at our house and Sheldon is home, I'll go get him so that you can meet him," Joan said.

"OK," I said.

After that day, whenever I was at their house, I would ask if he was home or if they had seen him. Finally the day came when I did not have to ask that question. As soon as I approached them, Lillie said, "Yes, he's home."

"Why don't you go ask him to come over here?" I said.

"No," said Lillie. "Joan, why don't you go?"

"All right," Joan replied.

A bit later Lillie and I were sitting on the wooden railing of the porch with our feet dangling as we watched Joan and Sheldon walk toward us. Wow, he was cute.

Joan said, "Sheldon, this is Jo-Ann. Jo-Ann, this is Sheldon."

We smiled at each other and simultaneously said, "Hi."

He sat down on the other side of me, and Joan continued to stand in front of us.

"Where do you live?" he asked.

"I live on Liberty Street."

"Who are your parents?"

"I don't have any parents here."

"What do you mean?"

"I live with the Johnsons."

"Are they your relatives?"

My eyes squinted, and with my head down, I replied, "No. They are not my relatives." There was silence for several seconds.

"Are you adopted?" Sheldon asked.

"What do you mean?"

"I thought that since they are not your relatives, maybe you were adopted and the Johnsons are your family now."

"No, I don't think they adopted me. All I know is that I was living in a Catholic girl's home, and the next thing I knew I was being sent here to live with them. No one mentioned adoption to me."

I had no idea what he meant by adoption and did not want to ask. "What about your parents?" I asked.

"I live with my mother," he replied.

He did not mention his father, nor did I.

His house was larger than Mrs. Johnson's. "You live in a big house." I said.

"We live downstairs, and another family lives upstairs."

Then he said, "Look, I have something to do, so I have to go. Jo-Ann, I'll see you the next time you come over here. Maybe you can come over to my house."

The smile on my face spoke volumes. "OK."

"See you," he said.

"See you."

I watched him walk back across the street and run up the steps into his house. That was the first time I had ever spoken with a boy who was not my classmate.

"Are you satisfied now?" Joan laughed.

I smiled and happily said, "Yes, I am."

Sheldon was constantly on my mind after that day, and I continued to look for him every morning I went to school. One morning, to my surprise he saw me and waved. I was so excited that he noticed me that I almost forgot to wave back and continued to watch him until he was no longer in sight.

My disobedience continued. I could not stay away from Van Buren Street because now I had an additional reason for going over there. One afternoon while I was at Joan and Lillie's house, Sheldon came over.

"Hi," he said.

We acknowledged him with, "Hi."

"Do you want to come over to my house?" he asked.

"Well, I am not sure. Is your mother home?" I asked.

"Yeah, she's home."

"OK." I motioned to Joan and Lillie to accompany me.

"No. We will wait here," said Joan.

"I don't want to go by myself. Please, please, come with me," I begged.

"We will go this time," Joan said.

"My mother wants to meet you," Sheldon said.

I wondered why his mother wanted to meet me. He must have told her something about me, even though he did not know me that well.

"OK," I said.

When we walked into his home, his mother was in the kitchen. When she heard us, she joined us in the living room.

Sheldon said, "Mom, this is my new friend, Jo-Ann. And these are the girls who live across the street, Joan and her sister, Lillie."

"Hello, girls," she said.

In unison, we replied, "Hello, Mrs. Brown."

"Please sit down." The three of us sat on the couch. "Would you like a slice of apple pie with milk or soda?"

"No, thank you," I said.

Joan and Lillie looked at each other, and when I saw their reaction, I wondered if I had responded too soon. Mrs. Brown took my response to be for the three of us.

She had a beautiful smile on her face, and her eyes glistened when she spoke to us. I immediately liked her.

"What's your last name, Jo-Ann?" asked Mrs. Brown.

"My last name is Cave."

"I don't know any Caves who live around here."

I reluctantly replied, "I live with the Johnsons."

"Where do you live?"

"I live with the Johnson family on Liberty Street."

"Oh, that's nice," she said. "Are you girls sure you don't want a slice of pie and something to drink?"

This time I responded, "Yes, please." And when I saw the smile on the sisters' faces, I knew I had made the right decision.

"Come sit at the kitchen table," Mrs. Brown said.

We followed her into the kitchen.

"Would you like soda or milk?"

I had never had soda before, so I spoke up first. "Soda."

Mrs. Brown gave each of us a slice of pie and poured us a glass of soda, which looked like chocolate milk but tasted better. That pie and soda were delicious. Sheldon was sitting at the table with us, so I tried not to gobble up my pie so fast. Prior to that day, I had not eaten apple pie, either. I wondered why we never had apple pie at Sacred Heart, since there was a huge apple orchard. We ate a lot of applesauce and baked apples but never apple pie. Why not? Maybe they would have had to make too many for us.

In silence, we enjoyed the pie and soda Mrs. Brown had prepared for us. She stood at the stove, stirring something with an aroma that filled our nostrils and reawakened our taste buds. That aroma was so good that I could have eaten any meal she cooked. Sheldon must have liked every dish his mother cooked. When Mrs. Brown turned toward us with her pleasant smile, our eyes met. I felt a rush of calmness and gratitude. It was almost as if I felt what a mother-daughter connection could be. My relationship with Mrs. Johnson was different because she was so much older than Mrs. Brown. Mary Jane and I had not spent as much time together.

I wanted that slice of pie to last forever, but when it was gone, I very slowly drank what was left of my soda.

"I really have to get back home now," I said.

"I will walk you back across the street," Sheldon said.

"Jo-Ann, come back to visit me some time," said his mother. "You don't have to come only when Sheldon is here, either."

"Thank you, Mrs. Brown," I said as I was leaving.

Joan and Lillie also thanked her. They skipped down the steps, but I walked so that my time with Sheldon would last a little longer.

"Your mother is very nice," I said. "And she makes the best apple pie I ever tasted." How could I let him know that I had never eaten apple pie before?

"Thanks," was his response.

## CHAPTER TEN

# IS HE A MAN OF GOD?

I believe that Mrs. Johnson's friend who lived on Van Buren Street—the same block as my friends—told Mrs. Johnson whenever she saw me with Joan and Lillie. Mrs. Johnson was very disappointed with me and told Mary Jane that I continued to disobey her. Little did I know that Mary Jane had a surprise for me that she must have been planning for a while.

"Jo-Ann," she said, "since you continue to disobey my mother by going over to Van Buren Street, I have something for you to do that will keep you busy. Come with me."

"Where are we going?"

"We are going across the street."

"Across the street?"

Mary Jane did not answer, so I shrugged my shoulders and followed her to a gray building. The door was opened by a tall, swarthy, buxom woman with a huge smile.

"Come on in," she urged.

Mary Jane said, "Hi, Virginia."

"Hi," she answered.

"This is Jo-Ann."

The woman looked at me with a pleasant smile. "Hello, Jo-Ann."

"Hello," I replied.

"Please sit down."

The thick pillows almost swallowed me. The room was beautifully decorated with an arch-shaped doorway opening into the dining room. Although Mrs. Johnson's home was larger, her home did not have a separate dining room. I later thought that maybe her dining room had been made into the living room and the living room made into the piano room, which made sense to me at the time.

"Jo-Ann, this is Mrs. Fitzgerald. She and Rev. Fitzgerald would like you to baby sit for them two evenings a week—and on Saturday."

At that time I did not know what "reverend" meant. He was the first person I had heard called that. I was too embarrassed to ask, but knew I could probably ask Mrs. Johnson later. If not, I could look it up in a dictionary at school. Mary Jane never told me why Rev. and Mrs. Fitzgerald needed a babysitter on those days, but refusing to babysit was not an option.

"Jo-Ann, my husband and I have a little girl, who is upstairs in her crib. When she cries, she either needs her diaper changed or is hungry, and I will show you how to change her diaper and warm a bottle of milk for her."

Mrs. Fitzgerald's husband entered the room and said, "Hello."

"Honey, this is Jo-Ann from across the street. She lives with Mary Jane and is going to babysit for us," she said to him.

"That is wonderful! Jo-Ann, I am glad you will help us out."

"Jo-Ann, this is my husband, Rev. Fitzgerald," she said.

Rev. Fitzgerald looked at Mary Jane. "How are you?"

Mary Jane looked at him with a smile and said, "I am fine."

"How is your mother?"

"She is fine too. Thank you for asking."

Mrs. Fitzgerald was pleasant and had a pretty smile. I had never seen anyone with such white teeth. She looked to be expecting another child.

Mary Jane said, "Virginia, I will leave Jo-Ann here for a while so that you can show her around and explain what you want her to do."

"Thanks, Mary Jane," she said.

Mary Jane had found a way to keep me away from my friends.

Mrs. Fitzgerald took me upstairs to her baby's room, where the baby lay in her crib. She showed me how to lower the side of the crib and check the baby's diaper, which needed to be changed. She removed the wet diaper and showed me where to put the soiled diapers and where the clean diapers were kept. She showed me how to fold the diaper before putting it on her baby and pinning it on both sides.

"Jo-Ann," she said, "I am going to remove this diaper and want you to get another one, and I want to see you fold it and put it on the baby."

I folded it correctly, put it on the baby, and pinned it correctly on my first try.

"Good," she said.

We then went downstairs to the kitchen, and Mrs. Fitzgerald showed me how to warm the baby's bottle. There was a pot on the stove with water in it. As she opened the refrigerator door, she said, "Get one of the baby's bottles, loosen the top, place it in the pot, and turn on the stove. Once the water starts to bubble, remove it from the pot, take the top off, and put your little finger in it to check the milk. It should be warm but not hot."

Mrs. Fitzgerald demonstrated how it was to be done and let me feel the warm milk. Then we took it upstairs to her baby. Mrs. Fitzgerald turned the baby's head to the side, put a folded diaper next to the baby's head, and placed the bottle on it.

"See, Jo-Ann. It's not hard."

"All right," I replied.

Rev. and Mrs. Fitzgerald lived in a duplex house with side-by-side apartments. They lived on one side, and their neighbor was an elderly lady whom I never met. Their backyard could be seen from the kitchen window.

Money was never mentioned for my babysitting services, nor do I remember ever being paid. Maybe the money was given directly to Mrs. Johnson or Mary Jane who arranged my services for free.

I enjoyed babysitting at their house. Their baby slept most of the time.

I do not remember how long I had been babysitting for the Fitzgeralds when a very troubling thing began to happen. At times Rev. Fitzgerald would come home before his wife. He would enter whichever room I was in, pull up my blouse, and begin to fondle my breasts. As naïve as I was, I knew that was not OK. I would try to walk away or remove his hand, but he would say, "Don't be afraid. I won't hurt you." Later I would learn that he had indeed hurt me psychologically.

No matter how many times I said stop, he ignored me and continued. There was no escaping him. Whenever he and I would be in their home alone, I would stay in the baby's room to avoid him, but eventually he would come into the room anyway. Though I knew that what he was doing was wrong, I was afraid to tell anyone for fear they would not believe me. By that time I knew he was a minister—"a man of God." At Sacred Heart, I never had heard any of the girls say that Father Mann had done that type of thing. The only time we were in his presence was in church. We were never allowed to be around him at other times. Would anyone take an eleven-year-old child's word over that of an adult—especially one who dedicated his life to God?

In my mind, his wife was such a nice, loving person who I did not want to hurt. I put her feelings before my own. Also, I thought that if I told Mrs. Johnson or Mary Jane and they believed what Rev. Fitzgerald had been doing to me, they would blame me and return me to Sacred Heart.

During one of my babysitting sessions, a visitor arrived at their home. He looked to be in his late teens or early twenties. That day I learned the visitor was Rev. Fitzgerald's brother, Carl. I do not know where Carl lived, but sometimes he would come to the house when I was babysitting. He was very friendly and would talk with me about school and my favorite subjects—which at the time were spelling and geography. Once he learned that I loved to spell, whenever he was at his brother's home, we would play spelling games. Carl would ask me to spell a word, or sometimes he would spell a word and ask me to pronounce it. One word in particular that he asked me to pronounce was "unique." I had mispronounced that word several times before giving up, and he told me how to correctly say it. That was a word I would never forget. I enjoyed our spelling games, and they improved my spelling and vocabulary. Carl was a very friendly person with whom I felt safe and comfortable.

On one of his visits, we were in the living room, and I stared at him with a strange look on my face.

"What's the matter, Jo-Ann?" he asked. I did not answer him. "Jo-Ann, I have never seen that look on your face before. What's that all about?"

"Something has been happening, but I am afraid to tell you about it."

"You can tell me anything. Don't be afraid," he said.

"If I tell you, will you promise not to tell anybody?"

"What is it?"

"First you have to promise not to tell anyone else—not even Mrs. Fitzgerald."

"All right. I promise I won't tell anyone."

Almost in tears, I asked, "Are you sure?"

"Jo-Ann, I said I won't tell anyone. Now what is it?"

I could not look at his face but managed to say, "Well...well." My voice quivered as I tried to find the right words.

"Well, what, Jo-Ann? What is it that you want to tell me?" he coaxed.

"Well, whenever I am over here and Rev. Fitzgerald comes home, he lifts up my blouse and rubs his hands over my chest."

"What?"

"I try to pull my blouse down, but he does it anyway."

Carl tried to lift my chin, and tears slowly rolled down my face. "Look at me, Jo-Ann."

I continued to resist eye contact. My face felt warm. I do not know how much time passed when he said, "You don't have to look at me, but tell me how many times he has done this to you."

"A lot of times—in the kitchen, in the baby's room, once in his bedroom."

"In his bedroom?"

"Yes, he pushed me down on the bed, and when I tried to get up, he pushed me back down. He does that whenever Mrs. Fitzgerald is not here," I replied.

"What else has he done?"

"He didn't do anything else. He does the same thing all the time and told me not to tell anyone."

Carl stood up, paced back and forth, rubbed his hands together, and wiped his forehead. His pace seemed to increase, but he did not say a word for several minutes. I knew he believed me. I felt so relieved that he believed me.

"Jo-Ann, now I am asking you to promise me something," Carl said.

"What is it?" I asked.

"Don't tell anyone else about this, not even the Johnsons. I will take care of this and will make sure it never happens again. Believe me. It will not happen again," he said in an elevated voice. "Jo-Ann, I am sorry you experienced such awful behavior from my brother. You should never have had to experience such a thing."

With my head lowered and tears welling in my eyes, I said, "Carl, thank you for believing me."

"Look, Jo-Ann, why don't you go upstairs, wash your face, and then go home. I'll watch the baby until my brother and his wife come home."

"Are you sure I should go home now? I do not want Mrs. Fitzgerald or her husband to be mad with me." I said.

He assured me that it would be OK. Crossing the street to go home, I felt so relieved that I was able to tell Carl my secret. I was glad that I told him and not Mrs. Johnson or Mary Jane, because I believed their reaction would have been much different.

After I divulged my secret to Carl, Rev. Fitzgerald never touched me again. Carl never mentioned to me what he had said to his brother, but whatever he said worked. From that day forward, whenever I babysat, I stayed in the living room with the baby. When I was upstairs in the baby's room and heard a door open or close, I would immediately take her downstairs with me.

Rev. Fitzgerald was the first minister I had ever met. When I first learned what he did, I thought of him the same way I did Father Mann. He was a holy man, and I admired them because they were men of God. In my religious teachings, I was taught that holy men followed the word of God and would do no wrong. Prior to my moving in with the Johnson family, Father Mann was the only religious man I had known. The only times Father Mann was in our presence was during religious functions, so I believed that was his only duty as a priest.

However, after my negative experiences with Rev. Fitzgerald, I never again felt comfortable in the presence of ministers or priests, because I feared they could not be trusted. We went to confession to confess our sins, and I always wondered whether or not Rev. Fitzgerald confessed his sins. If persons of the Catholic faith had to confess their sins to priests, to whom did priests and ministers confess their sins? The answer to that question was unknown to me, but I often wondered if Rev. Fitzgerald ever asked God's forgiveness for what he had done.

## CHAPTER ELEVEN

# PART OF MY YOUNG LIFE ENDED

One evening while I was enjoying *Hopalong Cassidy*, my favorite western television show, Mary Jane walked into the living room with a boy who was younger than me.

"Hi, Jo-Ann," she said and then walked to the kitchen.

I could not hear what was being said between them, but when their conversation was over, Mary Jane and the boy returned to the living room.

"Jo-Ann, I want you to meet Terry, who will be living with us," she said.

Terry was a little, skinny kid about five years old. Neither Mary Jane nor Mrs. Johnson explained why Terry was brought home to live with us nor how long he would stay. They probably thought they did not owe a child an explanation. As the child, I did not think I was supposed to ask for one. He was given the empty bedroom upstairs next to mine. Terry and I got along well together, and although I had many questions, I never asked him where he came from or why he was living with us. He might not have known anyway.

After having lived with the Johnsons for two years and several months, one afternoon upon my return home from school, I was given the surprise of my life. Mary Jane was sitting at the kitchen table. She was never at home when I returned from school. I placed my books on the table in preparation for doing my homework.

The first thing Mary Jane said to me was, "Jo-Ann, go upstairs and get all your things together."

"What do you mean?"

"Pack your clothes and other things you want to take with you."

"Why? Where am I going?"

"I am taking you back to Sacred Heart today."

"Did I do something wrong?"

"Jo-Ann, do not ask me anymore questions. Just go upstairs and get your things together."

"OK, but can I go say good-bye to Joan and Lillie?"

"That won't be necessary."

When I saw Mary Jane's wrinkled forehead and dipped eyebrows, I did not say another word. And although her face was frozen, I was able to hear words come from her almost-closed lips.

"Terry, go play in the backyard," she said.

Terry skipped to the backdoor. I thought about Terry having lived with us for just a few months. Why was he able to stay, but I had to leave? I broke my silence.

"Why do I have to leave?"

Mary Jane did not answer.

"Can I go say good-bye to Joan and Lillie?"

"No. Do not ask me that again."

"Are you taking me back because Joan and Lillie are my friends?"

Mary Jane's eyes widened, and she stared at me as if she could see through me. She stood up, looked directly into my eyes, and said in a more determined voice, "Do not ask another question. Just hurry up and do what you were told!"

Mary Jane never gave a reason or explanation about why I was kept from my friends and was not able to say good-bye. Joan and Lillie were my best friends. We had become so close. I do not believe I had felt that kind of hurt before—not even when I left Sacred Heart to live with the Johnson family. Why were grown-ups so mean? It would not have taken long for me to run over to Joan and Lillie's house. I just wanted to say good-bye. Not only was I leaving my best friends, but I was being taken away from the only home I had known.

I did what I was told and returned to the kitchen to talk with Mrs. Johnson. Tears rolled down my cheeks as I thought about all the times I had sat in the kitchen and watched her cook or iron clothes as she explained the correct way to fold them. My biggest regret was not continuing my piano lessons. I believe Mrs. Johnson enjoyed teaching me to play the piano just as much as I enjoyed learning as long as it did not interfere with my playtime. She was the grandmother I never had.

My only words to her were, "Good-bye, Mrs. Johnson. Thank you for letting me live here with you."

"That's all right, child. I am going to miss you." She hugged me and said, "Be a good girl."

Before that day, Mrs. Johnson had never hugged me, but she had always made me feel welcome in her home. I knew I would miss the times I had spent watching her wash clothes and tagging along carrying the clothespin bag as she hung them on the clothesline. Those clothes she hung on the clothesline were so white that they reminded me of clouds flying in the wind against a scenic background. During the times she performed those tasks, we talked. I considered those the most enjoyable times we spent together. She had not only taught me how to iron and fold clothes but had also given me the opportunity to deliver the clothes and get paid. Wow! That was my first paying job.

My ride back to Sacred Heart was quiet and lonely. I stared through the car window, full of thoughts of all the good times I had experienced with my friends and the Johnson family. My mind was so full of good thoughts that I was unable to see anything outside the window. But once I saw that Sacred Heart redbrick wall, reality was back. I still felt sad for not being allowed to say good-bye to my friends and for leaving the only home I had ever known. Mary Jane turned to look at me with an expressionless face.

When we arrived at Sacred Heart, she walked me to the door, which was opened by a nun. I was overwhelmed with sadness and unable to hear anything that was said between Mary Jane and the nun. There were no hugs or words spoken between us. I would not look at her because I did not want her to see my tears. When I heard the door close, I knew that part of my life had ended. There must not have been space available for me at Sacred Heart because shortly after my arrival, I was taken to another institution. That institution was Cardinal Hayes Convent Home in Millbrook, New York where I remained for a month. That was probably a holding facility until Sacred Heart had an opening. Nothing was ever told or explained to me about the reason for my stay there. However, I do remember that the nuns there wore long, brown habits with a large, wide head covering with a veil. I resided at that home for twenty-five days before being returned to Sacred Heart. There is nothing memorable about my stay at that facility. I do not remember a building, a day, an incident, a nun, or any other person for that matter. Maybe I was so heartbroken about having left the Johnson family that I blocked everything out once I was returned to Sacred Heart.

After my return to Sacred Heart, I often wondered if Terry had been brought into the Johnson home as my replacement. I wondered if Mary Jane had adopted him. Maybe twelve was too old, or maybe Mary Jane really did not want a girl. Maybe I was sent back because I disobeyed and continued my friendship with Joan and Lillie, or perhaps they knew about my new friend, Sheldon. All kinds of thoughts went through my mind, and I asked myself all kinds of questions that I knew would never be answered.

Most of the girls I had known before leaving Sacred Heart were still there when I returned—along with some new faces. Those I knew were glad to see me and asked a lot of questions about where I had spent the past two years and why I had returned. Usually when a girl left Sacred Heart Orphan Asylum, she did not return. It did not take me long to get back into my old routine of telling stories; however, I did not have to exaggerate as much to make my new stories interesting. I told them stories about the Johnson family, the house I lived in, Joan and Lillie, Sheldon, television programs I watched, music I listened to, and learning to dance. Also I told them about attending a school with boys and girls. The only person I did not mention in any of my stories was Rev. Fitzgerald. I never wanted anyone to know about him. Although I had plenty of interesting stories to tell, I was unable to tell the reason for my return and never tried to invent one.

After I had been back for a couple of weeks and the initial hurt of being returned eased, I wrote a letter to Joan and Lillie to let them know what had happened to me and how much I missed them. At night I would lie in bed thinking about the good times we had together and cry myself to sleep. I continued to portray myself as happy and joyous, but I hurt inside because of my loss of home and friends.

Joan and Lillie must have told Sheldon and his mother that I had been returned to the home when they received my letter, because I never did. About a month after my return to Sacred Heart, I was surprised one Sunday afternoon by Sister Augustina informing me that I had visitors. I thought the visitors might be Mary Jane and her mother, but I was more excited to see Mrs. Brown and Sheldon when I walked into that room.

I hugged Mrs. Brown and then Sheldon. I had never hugged Sheldon before, but I felt comfortable doing it at the time. We walked around the grounds, because I knew the girls would be on the playground and I wanted them to see me with my visitors. After I showed them around, we sat on a bench near the grapevines. I felt so special that day. That visit meant more to me than Sheldon or his mother would ever know. Sheldon looked good. He wore a plaid shirt, black pants, and gray cap. I do not remember ever seeing him without his cap. It was hard for me to believe Mrs. Brown had driven all the way to Sacred Heart with Sheldon just to visit me. She had always made me feel comfortable at her home, but I would never have thought she would do this. She was a very kind and caring person, so I guess I should not have been surprised. During the time I lived in Kingston, I never saw Mrs. Brown drive, and I did not know if she owned a car. That day was the best and happiest Sunday that I had ever experienced at Sacred Heart Orphan Asylum, because I had visitors I cared about and knew they cared about me.

After Mrs. Brown and Sheldon left and I had joined the other girls, right away they wanted to know what my visitors had brought me. They were expecting me to show them candy, cookies, books, or other material things, but what I received that day meant more to me than any material thing could ever mean. It was a precious gift that would remain in my heart. Mrs. Brown and Sheldon had shown me that they cared about me. Before my return to Sacred Heart, I had not spent too much time with Mrs. Brown, but that day she made me feel as if I had known her for years.

I was so excited about the visit, that same day I wrote a letter to Mrs. Brown thanking her for coming to see me. I wrote about how much their visit meant to me. I was so happy and excited during their visit that I was unable to verbally share my thoughts and feelings with them. Never in a million years would I have expected to receive a visit from Mrs. Brown and Sheldon. During my excitement, I decided to write a letter to Mrs. Johnson and Mary Jane. I thanked them for allowing me to live with them. In the letter, I told them about my visit from Mrs. Brown and Sheldon. I later thought that my writing to the Johnsons was a mistake, because Mrs. Brown and Sheldon never visited me again.

It was my belief that Mary Jane had something to do with my not receiving any more contact from the Browns. I thought she probably wrote to or called Mother Superior. I do not know what she would have written or said, but whatever it was prevented me from receiving any more visits. For the rest of my stay at Sacred Heart, Sundays were never as meaningful. A little of my time during all of those Sundays was spent thinking about that very special one. Mother Superior probably wrote Mrs. Brown to inform her that she could not return to visit me.

I wrote to Mrs. Brown, Sheldon, Joan, and Lillie several times but never received a response. I don't even know if my letters were ever mailed. We were not allowed to seal the envelopes of the letters we wrote. We had to place our letters in a box to be read before they were sent. Since I was never given letters, I assume that no one had written to me.

## CHAPTER TWELVE

# FAMILY

Much of my time at Sacred Heart was spent feeling sorry for myself because I did not receive visitors or letters. What made that time especially difficult was when other girls asked if I had a family. I would tell them that I had a mother. When they asked why she did not visit me, I made up tales such as she moved or she no longer had a car or whatever came to my mind at the time. I was good at making up excuses, but it did not erase the hurt. Although there were many other girls who did not have visitors, at that time I did not realize that they might be feeling the same loneliness and pain I did. I was so wrapped up in my own feelings that I was unaware of anyone else's suffering.

My only memory of my mother during my childhood was of the day she took me to the Sacred Heart Orphan Asylum. It bothers me that I cannot remember anything before that day. For the first thirteen years of my life, I virtually had no family. There were times I asked myself if the woman who had left me at Sacred Heart was indeed my mother because I had such a clear recollection of her on that day but nothing before then. It was difficult for me to understand how a parent could leave a young child at the door of an institution and, except for one visit, not look back. At times during my childhood, it was less painful for me to pretend that my mother did not exist than to think she did not want me. I always wondered what it would be like to have a mother, father, sisters, and brothers—because that was my image of a family. As I grew older, a family meant having any relative or relatives who loved me and cared about my well-being.

The eighth grade was the highest grade taught at the Sacred Heart. Once that grade was completed, girls were allowed to go home with their parents if they had them. If not, arrangements were made to send them to another home. My last year at Sacred Heart was lonely. Something was missing. I should have been happy that I would soon leave that place and never return, because for many years, that was exactly what I wanted, but suddenly I no longer felt that way.

The closer graduation day came, the more anxious I became. I was apprehensive about leaving, because I had no idea where I would be sent to live or with whom. I was sad because I was not allowed to communicate with anyone outside of Sacred Heart. Most eighth graders were excited and talked about where they would go or what they would do after graduation. My anticipation was of a different nature. I still had not heard from or received any recent visits from my mother. My mind actively tried to make sense of things. I thought maybe my mother did not want me and gave me away. Maybe that was the reason I was sent to live with the Johnson family, but they had not wanted me either. It seemed that no one wanted me.

Immediately after graduation, some girls left with their parents. Others who were planning to leave stayed to celebrate at a special picnic luncheon with those of us who were not leaving. The sun shone brightly on many happy faces that day. Although we were all happy to graduate, some of us were concerned because of the uncertainty in our futures. The girls with the biggest smiles and loudest laughter knew they were going home, but the rest of us had no idea when or where we would go.

Our celebration was held in the area where we sometimes played and had our May Day celebration. We celebrated our graduation as we did on May Day, with several maypoles with different colored ribbons hanging from the top of each pole. Each of us held a ribbon. Then, with music playing, we danced around the maypole, weaving over and under the girl in front of us. By the time the music ended, the pole was braided with a beautiful array of colors. After the maypole dance, we sat on wooden benches and recited the same grace said before every meal: "Bless us, oh, Lord, for these thy gifts which we are about to receive from thy bounty through Christ our Lord, Amen." We then consumed the food and beverages provided. We stayed outside to talk and play longer than normal on that day. The girls who knew their future addresses exchanged them with each other and also gave them to those of us who didn't have that information. My happiness slowly dwindled with the crowd, because I realized that I would never see nor hear from many of those girls again.

After graduation day, little by little, the graduated girls left Sacred Heart Orphan Asylum. Some went home with their parents, and we were told that some were sent to other orphan homes to live. One afternoon while I was removing dishes from the dining-room tables, Mother Madeline entered and said, "Jo-Ann, Mother Superior wants to see you in her office. Leave those dishes and go to her office right away."

*Oh, no, not again*, I thought. *What did I do this time?*

Upon my arrival to the dimly lit office, I found a short, stocky, white woman with shoulder-length, black curly hair and strawberry-red lips. She was sitting in one of the wooden chairs farthest from the door.

"Jo-Ann, Mrs. Hawley is your aunt, and she is here to take you home with her," said Mother Superior.

I nervously began to fidget and looked down. I stuttered and gulped, "I'll...I'll be leaving here to live with her?"

"Yes. Today you will be leaving with Mrs. Hawley, who is your aunt," Mother Superior replied.

*She can't be my aunt. She is white,* I thought. Why was I going to live with her? I was confused and wondered why my mother had not come to get me. She was the person who had left me at the home nine years earlier. I stood silently in front of Mother Superior's desk with my head lowered, tugging on both sides of my dress.

Then I asked, "Where's...where's my mother? Why didn't she come to get me?"

Mrs. Hawley smiled a nervous smile and said, "Your mother is in Florida. You will be living with your uncle and me for a few weeks before joining your mother."

"My uncle? I did not know I have an uncle."

"Yes, your uncle Nicholas is your mother's brother."

For nine years, I did not have a family, and now at the age of thirteen, I learned that I had an aunt and uncle. Did they know that I existed? Where were they during the past nine years? Why didn't they care enough to write to me, visit me, or let me live with them? I was sent to live with strangers instead of my own family. All of this was very confusing and disturbing to me. The unanswered questions of why my family never visited me at Sacred Heart became an obsession for me. They ran like a perpetual loop through my mind. This woman whom I was meeting for the first time was my aunt. She had come to take me away from Sacred Heart Orphan Asylum and told me I had an uncle that I did not know about. I flopped down into the chair but instinctively jumped up when I realized what I had done.

"That is all right. Sit down, Jo-Ann," Mother Superior said in a soft, pleasant tone that I had not heard from her before. She even had a smile on her face. I stared at her in disbelief—but I did obey. At that moment I wondered if she was nice to me because my aunt was there or because she was glad I was leaving or both.

"Can I say good-bye to the other girls?" I asked.

"No. Your aunt is ready to take you home."

Mother Superior seemed to be in a good mood, and I would be leaving soon, so why not try my luck?

"I would like to say good-bye and get some of my things," I pressed.

Mother Superior looked agitated.

"No. You won't need any of those things," Mother Superior said sternly.

"Jo-Ann can bring some of her clothes and whatever else she wants to bring. We have not bought any clothes or anything else for her yet," said Mrs. Hawley.

I immediately liked her because she was not afraid to speak up to Mother Superior. With a big smile on my face, I said, "I have to get some of my things and the addresses of some of my friends."

That was the first time I had ever spoken to Mother Superior with my head held high and such determination in my voice.

"Jo-Ann, tell Sister Augustina to give you a box to put your belongings in and hurry back. Do not keep your aunt waiting," Mother Superior said.

"Sister, I don't mind waiting. I know Jo-Ann wants to say good-bye to her friends," Mrs. Hawley said.

When my aunt said those words, I had gotten up from my chair and rushed to the door. Wow! I was allowed to say good-bye to my friends and give away some things. At that time, I was unable to give anyone my address, because I did not know it. I never knew why girls were not allowed to say good-bye, and I believed it was a dumb, hurtful policy that was never explained. Not being allowed to say good-bye before leaving the home was almost like a punishment for having lived there. Most of us never wanted to live there but did not have a choice in the matter. On the other hand, maybe the nuns thought it would be too upsetting for those who were not able to leave. We were never told the reasons for their decisions. Some of my closest friends had already left the home. They had given away some of their belongings before graduation day and their departure. I wondered why Mother Superior or Sister Augustina had not previously told me the day I was to leave.

I was led toward those big, wooden doors once again, but this time was different. All the other times, I had hurriedly walked toward those doors to get outside. This time I walked slowly and felt some sadness because I was leaving something certain for a new uncertainty. Once we were outside, I stopped for a moment and looked back at those big, heavy doors close off a part of my life. But, I was thankful that my aunt had made it possible for me to say good-bye that day.

Uncle Nicholas and Aunt Madeline lived in Poughkeepsie, New York, which was approximately seven miles from Sacred Heart Orphan Asylum in West Park. I would later learn that he was at work the day Aunt Madeline came to get me from Sacred Heart. She could not drive but was driven to the home by someone else. Uncle Nick was not yet home from work when we first arrived. Aunt Madeline showed me around the house and took me to the room that was to be my bedroom.

"Do you want to watch television?" she asked.

I responded by nodding my head yes.

"Your Uncle Nick should be home soon," she said.

I was sitting in the living room watching television when this tall, good-looking white man with straight brown hair entered the room. He wore black-rimmed glasses.

"You must be Jo-Ann," he said as he approached me. "I'm your uncle Nicholas, but you can call me Uncle Nick. I am your mother's brother."

He took my hand, pulled me from the chair, and gave me a hug. That was the first time I remember being hugged by a family member. Uncle Nick's skin color was whiter than Aunt Madeline's and just as white as or whiter than many white people I had previously seen.

"I would have picked you up from the home, but I had to work today," he said. "Jo-Ann, you'll be living with us for a couple of months before you're sent to Florida to live with your mother."

I had not known my mother was living in Florida prior to being told so by Aunt Madeline. My mother had never written to inform me of her whereabouts or anything else.

My second day living with my aunt and uncle was exciting. Aunt Madeline took me shopping and bought clothes for me. I had never been shopping before, and I enjoyed it just as much as she did. That shopping trip turned out to be one of many. She would call a cab to take us to the shopping area, and then we shopped. I knew her taste in clothes was great because she was always impeccably dressed. Though she had no children of her own, she did not have any problem picking out and buying nice clothes for me. Those afternoons of shopping meant so much to me, and I believe she enjoyed them just as much as I did. On those shopping trips, we would shop until we were tired, sit down to rest, and then shop some more. Many afternoons when we did not shop, Aunt Madeline would play records by her favorite artist, Billie Eckstine, while enjoying a glass of scotch and water.

Aunt Madeline was very attractive. She did not work. She was charismatic and had beautiful clothes, furs, and jewelry that she wore well. She looked immaculate at all times—with never a hair out of place. Uncle Nick and Aunt Madeline lived with their dog in a nice apartment complex on Green Street.

I had never seen two people more in love. Whenever Uncle Nick walked into the house, the first thing he would do was kiss Aunt Madeline. He doted on her every need. I felt a closeness to my aunt and uncle that I did not think was possible. They were my family and treated me as if I were their own child. I had always wondered what it would be like to have a real family, and they showed me. Although I enjoyed every moment I spent with Aunt Madeline, I felt much closer to and more comfortable with Uncle Nick. At times I thought Aunt Madeline felt a little uneasy around me. Maybe it was because she did not have children and did not know how to act or what to say.

When Uncle Nick was not at work, he would talk with me and show me family pictures. He showed interest in my feelings. A couple of times during our talks, I wanted to ask if he had known that I had been living at Sacred Heart Orphan Asylum and, if so, why he had not visited me. For some reason, I thought that if I asked those questions, it would jeopardize our relationship. I did not want to say or do anything that would risk causing such a disruption. Another reason for not asking those questions might have been because I was afraid of the answers he would give. So I never knew.

Uncle Nick talked with me about his mother—my grand-mother—who was another relative I had not known about. I was surprised one day when she came to visit him.

*Wow, I have a white grandmother too*, I thought.

She was very friendly and was interested in me and my progress in school. I showed her my large school scrapbook of accomplishments. It was full of test papers, artwork, and school newsletters containing articles I had written. I gave it to her. She was somewhat surprised but thanked me for it. That was the only time I saw my grandmother while at Uncle Nick's home. I also wondered if she had known where I lived for the past nine years.

During my stay at Uncle Nick's, I often wondered why he, Aunt Madeline, or my grandmother had never come to visit me at Sacred Heart. Uncle Nick and Aunt Madeline lived so close to West Park, which was where Sacred Heart was located. Over the years, I had thought my only family member was my mother, but I was wrong. Did they know about me? If they did know about me, why was I just finding out about them? I wondered why I was sent to live with the Johnson family when I had relatives of my own. Those were the questions I really wanted answered but was too afraid to ask.

I enjoyed my stay with Uncle Nick and Aunt Madeline and was able to enjoy the family experience that developed between us. One weekend Uncle Nick took me on a sight-seeing tour of Poughkeepsie. He drove by IBM, which was his place of employment, and we visited the Vanderbilt estate and other places he thought would be of interest to me. Often Uncle Nick would spontaneously say, "Come on, Jo-Ann. Let's go for a ride." I felt so special during those times he and I spent together. He was a kind, generous, and thoughtful man. Uncle Nick treated me the way I always dreamed of being treated by my mother or father. He was my father figure. Deep down inside, I hoped that he thought of me as the child he may have wanted and was able to experience a parent-child bond with me.

I awakened one morning to rays of the sun cascading through my open bedroom window along with a cool breeze carrying the melodic sounds of birds chirping. The sudden aroma of bacon widened my nostrils, but I could not tell if it was from within or outside of the house. When I got out of bed that morning, I was surprised to find Aunt Madeline cooking breakfast. She seldom did. Most mornings I ate a bowel of cornflakes—which I enjoyed.

Reality set in that morning when I joined Uncle Nick and Aunt Madeline at the breakfast table. My beautiful morning ended when I remembered that was the day I would leave their home. The breakfast Aunt Madeline cooked smelled good and looked delicious. I moved my fork through the scrambled eggs as if making a pathway to the bacon. The silence was finally broken when I heard Aunt Madeline say, "Eat your food, Jo-Ann; don't play with it." A lonely tear dropped onto my plate as I thought about eating my last meal with my aunt and uncle.

For the first time in my life, I had experienced what it was like to have a real, loving family, and that was about to be taken away from me. At least this time, I would not leave feeling empty. I would leave full of love and wonderful memories that would remain with me forever. Aunt Madeline and Uncle Nick were like a mother and father to me. Aunt Madeline had bought me a suitcase and helped me pack for the trip. Uncle Nick enjoyed my interest in him and my questions, and he enjoyed my telling him about living at Sacred Heart and with the Johnson family. He would ask me questions and show as much interest in my life as I did in his.

On our way to the train station, I broke the silence. "Uncle Nick, I don't want to go. Can I stay with you?"

"Jo-Ann, I wish you could stay with us, but your mother wants you to live with her."

I frowned and said, "I don't even know my mother. She never wanted me to live with her before. I want to stay here."

"You can write to us, and maybe you can come back to visit some time."

At that moment I knew that I could not change the outcome of my situation. My eyes welled up with tears.

"OK." I cried.

Uncle Nick and Aunt Madeline walked me onto the train and to my seat. I hugged them both but was unable to speak.

"Your mother will meet you at the station," said Uncle Nick.

They remained on the train with me as long as they could. When they got off the train, they stood outside my window and waved. I could see their silhouettes through my tears and waved back as the train slowly moved me away from that part of my life.

CHAPTER THIRTEEN

# ANOTHER MOVE

As I rode on the train, my feelings of despair and uncertainty were overwhelming, but anticipation of a new life with my mother awaiting me in Florida was unbelievable. I experienced different levels of excitement. The trip was my first train ride and my first time out of New York. I was traveling all the way from New York to Florida. What would life be like for me in Florida? I would live with my mother, whom I did not know or remember. My life before the day I was taken to Sacred Heart was a blank. I sobbed softly as different thoughts ran through my mind until I dozed off to sleep.

When I arrived at the Florida train station, I was met by a woman whom I believed was my mother and a man she told me was my uncle John. He put my suitcase in his car and drove us from the train station to Dania, Florida, located between Fort Lauderdale and Hollywood. She looked very different than I remembered from all those years ago. She was wearing a pair of shorts and a short-sleeved blouse. Her hair was long and pulled back in a ponytail. As soon as we were in the car, she lit a cigarette.

Their home was located on a dead-end street, where two duplex apartment buildings faced each other. Uncle John and his wife lived in the same apartment building as my mother but next door. Each apartment consisted of a living room, kitchen, two bedrooms, and one bathroom.

When I was introduced to Aunt Berenice, she got up from sitting in a rocking chair—I thought to shake my hand. I put my hand out, but she pulled me toward her and unexpectedly hugged me. I immediately liked her.

"I'm glad to finally meet you, Jo-Ann. You can sit down. Would you like something to eat or drink?" she asked as she walked toward the kitchen. "I know you had a long train ride and must be hungry."

"No, thank you," I replied even though I was hungry.

"Don't be shy. I cooked enough food to feed all of us and our neighbors. Come sit at the table, and I will fix a plate for you."

I did sit at the table and bowed my head before eating. The food smelled good and was very tasty. Although I was hungry and wanted to gobble up the food, I ate very slowly and was glad no one else sat at the table with me. I thought about all those days while at Sacred Heart when I watched other girls get visits from their family and cried because I did not have family to visit me. I had wondered why no one visited me and wished for a family. I had felt so alone then, but now my family had increased from just having a mother to a grandmother, two uncles, and two aunts. I had five additional family members whom I had never known existed. Where were they when I really longed for and needed them?

I wondered if the nuns knew about my family. Maybe that was why they sent me to live with the Johnsons. Maybe my mother was not the only family member who did not want me. After meeting my new family, over and over again I wondered if they had known about me and knew that I lived in an orphan asylum. If they knew of my existence, why did they let me remain at that place?

Aunt Berenice was a beautiful, light-skinned black woman. She wore her brown hair in one long braid that reached the middle of her back.

"How was your train ride?" she asked with a smile. At the time she asked that question, I had a mouth full of food, so I hurriedly chewed and swallowed before I answered her. The nuns had taught us to never talk with food in our mouths.

"It was all right. I slept most of the way."

Uncle John had smooth, dark-ebony skin. A tooth edged in gold appeared when he smiled. Their daughter, Edythe's, skin complexion was similar to her father's. Edythe walked into the room and said, "Hi, Jo-Ann, I'm Edythe, but you can call me Wimpy. Everyone calls me that—it's my nickname," she said.

She was five years older than me and had just graduated from high school. Aunt Berenice prepared a plate of food for Uncle John, who joined me at the table. I wished I had eaten faster so that I would have been finished before he sat down.

"How's the food?" he asked.

"It is very good," I replied.

As soon as Uncle John's plate was prepared, he began to eat without saying grace. I completed my meal without uttering another word. Once I finished eating, I stood up from the table.

"Jo-Ann, just put your plate in the sink. Wimpy will wash the dishes later," Aunt Berenice said.

I had not left a single morsel on my plate. The nuns would not let us leave any food on our plates, regardless of whether we liked it or not.

After I had eaten, I sat on the couch. Peggy Sue, their small, black and white dog, nudged my leg, and I petted her. She then lay down by my feet and became my new friend.

After we sat and they talked for a while, my mother must have sensed my uneasiness. "Why don't you come next door and unpack your things?" she suggested.

"Thank you for the food," I said as I got up to leave.

"You don't have to thank me," Aunt Berenice said.

My mother showed me around her apartment, ending the tour in my bedroom, where I remained to unpack. I placed my suitcase on the bed and removed my clothes—piling them on the bed. Once they were organized, I placed them inside the dresser drawers in that order.

Tears rolled down my cheeks as I sat on the side of the bed. I looked at the two large windows that flooded the room with light and airiness. One window was in the same wall as the bed's headboard, and the other was on the opposite side of the bed. The closet was located toward the foot of the bed, which was to the right of the door. That bedroom was smaller than the one I'd had at the Johnsons' house but larger than the one at Uncle Nick's. My bedroom could have fit three beds and two chairs from Sacred Heart's dormitory.

I could not think about Sacred Heart without thinking of that one particular morning when I had experienced that terrible accident so many years earlier. The humiliation I had suffered that day was probably why I never wet the bed again. In addition to that incident,

I thought of my friends and the various moves I had made over the past several years. Oh, how I wished I could have stayed with Uncle Nick and Aunt Madeline, but now that I was here, I hoped the move to Florida would be my last. When I heard footsteps approaching my room, I wiped away the tears.

My mother stood in the doorway and asked, "Do you want to come into the living room so we can talk?"

Without looking in her direction I responded, "No, thank you."

"Do you want something else to eat or drink?"

"No, thank you. I am full. I just want to stay in here for a while."

"All right, but if you want anything, let me know," she said as she walked away.

I stayed in my room for quite some time before making the decision to join her. Smoke reached my nostrils before I reached the living room. When I walked into the room, my mother was sitting in a chair with her legs crossed and holding an ashtray in one hand and a cigarette in the other. A package of cigarettes was on the small table. Without saying a word, I sat down on the sofa next to the armrest farthest from her. I do not know why I made the decision to sit in that location, but I do know it was not because of the smoke.

"How was your trip?" she asked.

That question had already been asked and answered at Aunt Berenice's house, but I responded—even though I did not remember anything about my train ride. "I slept most of the way. It was OK."

"How are your uncle Nick and Madeline doing?"

With a sense of pride upon hearing Uncle Nick and Aunt Madeline mentioned, I looked directly at her and said, "They are doing fine. I really enjoyed living with them."

She did not respond right away to my answer.

My eyes scanned the room, comparing it to Uncle Nick's living room. In comparison, the room was bleak with modest furnishings. There were no pictures on the walls and no curtains over the windows. I had never seen windows like those before, and later I learned that many homes in Florida had what they called jalousie windows. Those were individual slats of glass the length and width of a window. They could be turned outward and opened for ventilation. In addition to jalousie slats on windows, many front and back doors had them. The living-room linoleum tile was the same as the tile throughout the apartment. There were no rugs on the living-room floor. The kitchen table and three chairs were against the back wall of the living room. And the only thing that adorned the wall was a clock above that table.

While I was observing my surroundings, I heard, "Does Madeline work?"

Surprised to hear that question, I answered, "No."

"I can remember when she worked at a tuberculosis sanatorium, but it didn't last long because Madeline did not want to work. Your uncle Nick told her to quit her job, and she has not worked since."

"If she does not want to work and Uncle Nick wants her to stay home, that is great. She is really nice. I like her," I said.

"Since I mentioned work, I work Monday through Friday and have arranged for you to spend weekdays next door at your aunt Berenice's house while I'm at work. Your aunt Berenice suffers with asthma and is expecting a baby, so she can use some help around the house. She will probably ask you to do some chores, such as wash and dry dishes, hang clothes on the clothesline, or remove the clothes when they are dry. Another thing she might ask you to do is to go to the store, which is about three blocks from here."

"OK."

Quietness again engulfed the room until she said, "Do you think you want to eat something now? I cooked spaghetti."

Although I had previously said I was not hungry, rather than hurt her feelings, I said, "All right, I will eat a little bit."

When she went into the kitchen to prepare the food, I sat against the back of the sofa and wondered why she had not asked me about how my time at Sacred Heart Orphan Asylum, or Cardinal Hayes Convent Home, or the home of the Johnsons had been. Did she even know about my stay at Cardinal Hayes Convent Home or the Johnsons? She didn't ask me anything about what my life had been like during the nine years we were separated. I was quite surprised that she did not even tell me about her life during that period. To me, that was more important than talking about Uncle Nick and Aunt Madeline or even chores I would have to do at Aunt Berenice's house. I hoped she would tell me about the things that were most important to me. But she did not, and I was either afraid or too stubborn to ask.

To my amazement, she returned with a full plate of spaghetti for each of us. She must have forgotten that I had eaten at Aunt Berenice's house a short time before. That was too much food. We sat at the table together, and still no questions were asked about my stay at Sacred Heart or anything said about our years of separation. I had never eaten spaghetti before. I tried to pick some up with my fork, but it was too long. Then I twirled it around and around on my fork to no avail. Finally feeling a little irritated, I cut the spaghetti with my knife and ate it.

She must have been amused at watching me struggle with the spaghetti, but never instructed me as to the correct or proper way to eat it. We ate in silence. I ate as much as I could, which was not very much. Then I stood up from the table and said, "Thank you. I have had enough."

"Scrape your food into the trash can, and put your plate in the sink. I will wash it later."

At Sacred Heart, we were not only forbidden to leave food on our plate but also not allowed to throw food away.

"Should I put this away for tomorrow?" I asked.

"You don't have to, because we have more than enough for tomorrow."

The nuns taught us that throwing away food was a sin. I felt very uncomfortable scrapping that food into the trash can. While staying with the Johnson family or Uncle Nick, I never threw away food.

Never looking at her, I asked, "You gave me too much food. Is it all right if I fix my own plate from now on?"

"Sure, if that is what you want."

From that day forward, I fixed my own plate of food, only putting on my plate as much as I knew I could eat. If I wanted more food, I got more, but I never threw any away.

Aunt Berenice had a rocking chair on her side of the porch. Later that evening after having eaten dinner, she looked through the window and said, "Pete, why don't you and Jo-Ann come out and sit with me for a while?"

My mother responded, "I'll be out in a few minutes. I have some things to do." That was how I found out my mother's nickname was Pete.

"I am going to get ready for bed," I said.

"It's still early. Go out and join your aunt Berenice for a while," my mother said.

Although I did not want to go outside, I did, and Aunt Berenice said, "Jo-Ann, go inside and get a chair, or you can sit on the step."

Without hesitation, I sat on the step. Peggy Sue, who had been lying next to Aunt Berenice's rocking chair, came over to sit next to me. I gently rubbed her back, and she lay down.

"Peggy Sue likes you, Jo-Ann," said Aunt Berenice. "She usually does not warm up to people like that. Now she will follow you all around the place."

"That's OK," I said with a smile as I continued to rub Peggy Sue's back.

Aunt Berenice made me feel at ease, which made it easy to like her. She told me about the weather in Florida and about the mosquitoes. She also told me about hurricanes they sometimes experienced and explained how they prepared for them. Before that time, I had never heard of hurricanes. The information she told me about hurricanes was interesting, exciting, and a little scary. We sat on the porch until after dark. My mother never did join us, but I did not realize that fact until it was time for me to go inside. However, I did enjoy the company of Aunt Berenice and Peggy Sue.

I believe the years we spent apart had a negative impact on the relationship between my mother and me. I truly never felt that I was my mother's child, because we did not have a mother-daughter bond. I felt closer to my aunt Berenice than I did my mother. My aunt and I spent a lot of time together, and many people thought she was my mother. They even said we looked alike.

For many years, my family had consisted of the nuns and girls at Sacred Heart Orphanage Asylum. There was no affection shown by the nuns, but they nurtured us, educated us, and provided us with a place to live behind those cold redbrick walls. They did more for me than any member of my family. The values and foundation instilled in me by the nuns of the Sacred Heart Orphan Asylum shaped who I became—my thinking and my development. There were many times I did not want to follow their instructions and would seethe, pout, mutter under my breath, or talk back when told to do something. However, at that time I did not realize they were creating a positive pathway that ultimately I would follow into my future. Today when I see an adult talking with a mouthful of food or sitting with elbows on the table while eating, I remember the nuns' teachings.

The excellent education I received at Sacred Heart was the stepping stone to achieving my future goals. The public schools I attended did not come close to meeting the standards of that parochial school.

The nuns, while putting up with disrespect from me, taught me the importance of respecting my elders. I talked back, called them names, made fun of them, and criticized them for no apparent reason. While putting up with my nonsense, they taught me tolerance and respect for others. Though I hated the nuns, believing they were very cruel, I later realized that the Catholic home provided me a foundation of values, discipline, and consideration of others. The nuns were indeed instrumental in providing me with beneficial life lessons. My closest girlfriends at Sacred Heart were like sisters. We shared our feelings, thoughts, and our secrets. At times we cried together, and we shared many laughs together. I do not know how I would have survived without them.

# PART II

# TEEN YEARS

## CHAPTER FOURTEEN

# NEW EXPERIENCES

A few weeks after my move to Florida, my cousin Wimpy decided she was going to curl my hair. A hot comb or curling iron had never been used on my hair. After my hair was completely curled, Wimpy said, "Jo-Ann go ahead and comb your hair."

I went into the bathroom, looked into the mirror, and began to comb my hair. By the time I finished combing, it looked as if I had stuck my finger into an electrical socket. I walked into the living room and was surprised by her remark.

She said, "Jo-Ann, what did you do? You weren't supposed to comb all the curls out!"

I felt so ashamed and embarrassed by her remarks. Wimpy knew that I did not know how to comb curls, because when she was straightening and curling my hair, I had told her I never had that done to my hair before. Her tone of voice was not only embarrassing, but hurtful, because she made those remarks in front of Aunt Berenice and one of her girlfriends. My hair was fine before she decided it needed straightening and curling.

My retort was loud and spontaneous. "I told you I never had my hair curled before, so how was I supposed to know the curls were not to be combed out?"

She heard the frustration in my voice and realized what she had done, Wimpy laughed and said, "Come here, Jo-Ann. Let me see what I can do with it."

"No. That's OK," I replied and returned to the bathroom. I remained in there for some time brushing my hair and finally put it in two braided ponytails. After that day, I never let her touch my hair again.

Uncle John was pretty cool. That was an expression I picked up from the kids at school. He worked two jobs. During the day, he worked at a place where screens for doors and windows were made. Some evenings and on weekends, he worked as a bartender at the American Legion Hall, which was located not far from where he lived.

I think he enjoyed the bartender job more than his day job. When old records were replaced on the hall's jukebox, Uncle John would bring them home. Uncle John and Aunt Berenice had lots of records at home, but I never saw or heard them play any of them. Before he would leave for the bar, he showered, dressed, and always smelled nice. Uncle John had lots of clothes and looked nice in them. Once he was dressed, he pranced around the house like a black stallion. I thought he hung around the house waiting for Aunt Berenice to give him a compliment before he would leave. Sometimes I believed she purposely withheld her compliment just to see how long he would prance around the house.

When he felt he had waited long enough for a compliment, he would say, "Toots, how do I look?" I never heard her comment negatively toward him. Most times she would say, "You look as sharp as a tack." Toots was Uncle John's nickname only for Aunt Berenice. He was the only person to call her by that name.

Some evenings Aunt Berenice would go to the bar and stay while he worked. Sometimes I wondered if she joined Uncle John because she was tired of being at home all day and night or if she was trying to keep an eye on him because there were times on the weekends when he did not return home until the next day.

## CHAPTER FIFTEEN

# SEGREGATED SOUTH

Attucks High School was the first all-black school that I had ever attended. Riding a bus to school was another first for me. All the children who rode the bus were black as well. Before my first ride on that bus, I heard Aunt Berenice talking about the bus driver, Mr. Shine, the owner of the bus who also owned a filling station. The first time I stepped onto that big, white bus, I noticed the bus driver—who was the darkest black man I had ever seen. He had a thick, black strap across his lap and threatened to use it on us if we misbehaved. Luckily I never saw him use it on anyone. At that time I did not know if Shine was his first name, last name, or a nickname. The fact that there were only black children who rode that school bus should have been a hint of what I would discover at school, but it was not.

None of the books I had read prior to moving to Florida prepared me for that unusual chapter in my life. At this point my attendance at Attucks High School was my initial experience of segregation. All the students' faces were like mine—perhaps a lighter or darker hue. When I moved in with my mother, I should have immediately realized the difference between living in Florida and New York. In Florida, there was not one white family in the neighborhood. When I lived with the Johnson family in New York, white neighbors lived on both sides of their home. White people lived on the entire block. Sacred Heart Orphan Asylum was filled with girls of all colors, nationalities, and origins. Segregation put an entirely new perspective on my life in Florida.

My eyes widened in disbelief as I walked through the halls of Attucks High School and saw different shades of black faces everywhere. Why were there no white or Hispanic kids at that school? The schools I had attended in New York had kids of all races. Neither my mother nor Aunt Berenice had mentioned the fact that I would be attending an all-black school. One would think they knew I had never attended an all-black school before. I thought it was important enough for them to mention, but it was just the way things were in those days in Florida. The weird expression on my face must have seemed strange to the other students, but I was in shock! Not only were all the students black, but so were the teachers. One thing was certain: I was living in a place different from any other I had known.

Most of the curriculum and content taught at that school were not new to me. I had been taught most of it at Sacred Heart. I was disappointed not to be learning anything new. I watched the way the other students dressed, communicated, and interacted with each other. This was an education for me, as well as entertainment. The other students made fun of the way I spoke and verbally mocked me in class. The instructors were not very sensitive to my plight—which made me think they enjoyed it. I did not make new friends at school right away. The few friends I did make lived in my neighborhood. I met them through Aunt Berenice. In order to be accepted by my classmates, I found myself trying to imitate the way they spoke with the accent and slang. The only students I even attempted to speak to were those who rode the school bus. Mostly my only exchange with them was, "Hi."

While I lived up north in Kingston and attended PS 8, whenever any of the kids asked me where I had previously attended school, my response was always the same: "Sacred Heart—an all-girls Catholic school." By the time I had moved to Florida, my response to that question had changed to, "I attended an all-girls parochial school in New York." For some reason, I thought the word "parochial" would be associated with class and sophistication. After hearing my response, they would ask, "What's a parochial school?" When I heard that, I knew they would believe whatever I said about school. However, I was surprised they did not know that a Catholic school and a parochial school were the same. My parochial-school response always made me feel good about myself, and I thought it made me look better in their eyes. Attending a boarding school meant that my parents could afford to pay for me to get the best education. At public school, I outperformed the other students anyway, so it was not difficult for them to believe I had received a better education.

I did not want anyone to know I was raised and schooled in an orphan asylum. If I had been able to conjure up the nerve to tell anyone that I was raised in an orphanage, I definitely would not have added the word "asylum" to it. In my perception, if the other kids had known that I was raised in an orphan asylum, they probably would have teased me with taunts of being an orphan and not having a family. They might have constantly made fun of me and called me crazy and insane, in addition to other hurtful names. "Orphanage" equaled no parents, and "asylum" was associated with insanity. There may have been other girls at Sacred Heart who did not have family, because many did not receive visitors. Also, like me, they may have had family who just did not visit them. Some of them could have suffered with mental problems, but I was unaware of them. At the time I did not associate the word "asylum" with refuge.

Algebra was my favorite class because it was new to me. It was much harder for me to learn—which I blamed on the teacher rather than the subject. A boy by the name of Lawrence was the first male student in any of my classes who stood out from the others. He was a good-looking, caramel-complexioned boy with a mesmerizing smile. Many of the boys in class tried to impress girls by being loud and obnoxious—but not Lawrence. He smiled, walked, and talked softly, and all the girls looked and listened.

One morning most of the students were laughing and talking as they usually did while awaiting the teacher's arrival. My method of blocking out the noise was to read a book. That day I momentarily looked away from my book to discover Lawrence looking over my shoulder with that big smile.

He asked, "What are you reading?"

"It's not algebra," I said as I closed the book and placed it face down on my desk. The book was titled *The Man Who Sold the Eiffel Tower*. I thought the book was very interesting, but I did not tell Lawrence its title.

He moved to the side of my desk. "You're not from around here, are you?"

"No. I am from New York."

"I knew you weren't from around here because you talk and act different."

"I may talk differently, but how do I act different?"

"Whenever I see you, you are alone and reading a book. The books are not always schoolbooks."

I smiled and replied, "So I like to read. What's wrong with that?"

"Nothing, but I never see you at any of the after-school events. Do you like sports or the school band?"

Before I could answer, he and the other students scurried to their seats. I wondered what his response would have been if I had told him I was not allowed to attend after-school functions. Uncle John and Aunt Berenice always told me to get directly on the bus after school and not to miss it. Every day when school was out, Mr. Shine and that big white bus were always waiting for us across the street. I do not remember anyone who rode the bus to school ever not riding it back home. Mr. Shine knew the parents of every child who rode his bus, even though he may not have known our names. If he had to wait an extra five or ten minutes for anyone to board the bus, he would inform that student's parents.

When I got home from school, I did my homework and then went next door. When not at school, I spent most of my time with Aunt Berenice. If Aunt Berenice was cooking, we talked about whatever it was she was cooking. She would instruct me on how to prepare certain foods. She taught me how to cut up onions without getting teary eyes and how to make gravy—among other things. I liked everything she cooked, but my favorite dish was stuffed peppers. Sometimes I would go to the store for her or go to Miss Daisy's house to take food or a message. Miss Daisy was an elderly woman in her late sixties or early seventies. She and her husband lived in the smallest house I had ever seen. It had four small rooms. Miss Daisy lived a block over from Aunt Berenice. There was a fence that prevented direct access to Miss Daisy's house, but I learned how to squeeze myself under the metal fence to keep from having to walk around the block. I later saw some of the neighborhood kids use that method for quicker access to where they wanted to go.

## CHAPTER SIXTEEN

# CLEVELAND

Dania Park was only a block from our home. The park's pavilion was not far from the street. Sometimes on my way to Green's store, I heard a whistle from the direction of the park, but I kept walking. On one occasion while on my way to the store, I heard a whistle and turned in its direction. I saw a boy who motioned for me to go over to where he was, but I continued to walk until I heard footsteps behind me. I turned around to notice that same boy almost beside me. His arms were huge, and his chest looked as if it were trying to escape confinement from under its T-shirt. He was not bad looking but not as cute as Lawrence.

"Hi, what's your name?" he asked.

I kept walking.

"I haven't seen you around here before," he said. "What's your name?"

He continued to walk with me, and I realized he was not going to leave me alone.

"My name is Jo-Ann."

"Are you new here?"

"Yes." I continued to the store with him beside me. He was a tall and powerfully built boy, who looked straight into my eyes when he spoke. I did not know what to say, but I finally asked, "What is your name?"

"Cleveland. Everybody calls me Cle. Where are you from?"

"New York."

"What part?"

"Poughkeepsie."

"I never heard of it."

I did not respond and walked into the store. After that day, whenever Cleveland saw me walking to the store, he joined me, and we talked.

One day he said, "You should ask your parents if you can come to the park some time."

"OK, I will," I said.

One afternoon on our way from the store, he walked me all the way home, and Uncle John saw him. When Cleveland left, my uncle told me he did not want me to see Cleveland again. He said Cleveland was Wimpy's age and too old to be hanging around with me. The next time I saw Cleveland, I told him what my uncle had said.

"Well, I won't walk you home anymore," was his response.

We continued to walk and talk whenever he saw me going to the store, but he did not walk me home. He would walk as far as the corner of my street and then turn toward the park.

"I'll see you later," he always said.

"OK," was always my reply.

One of my most memorable experiences with him happened on a Saturday. I woke up to the sun piercing my bedroom window, which immediately brought a smile to my face. Usually I'd wake up with anything but a smile and turn from the window to doze off. That morning was different from the others. The sun almost felt like a nutrient to my outstretched body. I did not have to be coaxed out of bed. My mother was in the bathroom, so I made up my bed and straightened my room. Once she came out of the bathroom, I hurriedly washed and prepared myself for the day. I ate a bowl of cereal, cleaned the kitchen, and made sure all my chores were done.

After completing my chores at home, I checked with Aunt Berenice. She told me to clean her kitchen and then hang some clothes on the clothesline. It seemed as if she always had clothes to hang or take down from the clothesline. For some reason, it seemed as if I had more chores than normal that day.

As soon as I finished, I asked, "Aunt Berenice, can I go to the park now?"

Her response was, "Jo-Ann, it's OK with me, but you should go ask your mother."

Those were words I didn't want to hear. I took a deep breath before approaching my mother, and with a pleasant tone, I said, "I finished cleaning my room, the kitchen and bathroom, and some things for Aunt Berenice. Can I go to the park now?"

"Yes, but be home before dark," she said.

"OK," was my response as I rushed out of the house and toward the park.

Cle was not at the park, so I walked to Miss Green's store, as we had previously planned. He was sitting behind the steering wheel of his father's car.

"I didn't know you could drive," I said.

"There are a lot of things you don't know about me," he said with a smile. "Get in. Let's go for a ride."

"I can't do that. If anybody sees me, I'll be in a lot of trouble."

"No one is going to see you. Get in and put your head down until I tell you it's OK to sit up."

When we reached the other side of town, I was able to sit up. I was glad no one saw me. He drove around different areas of town I had never seen. He made a complete stop when we reached the beach. We walked on the sand holding hands and found a spot to sit. Cle and I talked for what seemed like hours. Then I remembered I had to get back home. I stopped by Miss Daisy's house first. When I went to Miss Daisy's house, my routine was to ask if she needed anything from the store or if she had something she wanted me to take home to Aunt Berenice. The times she gave me baked goods or jam she had made were the most promising. I thought Aunt Berenice or my mother would believe that, in addition to spending time at the park, I had also spent my time away from home with Miss Daisy. That was not the only reason. Miss Daisy made the best pies, cakes, cookies, and jam I had ever tasted. I enjoyed every crumb and morsel. Although I ate some at Miss Daisy's home, I did not refuse any later when offered by Aunt Berenice. Miss Daisy's was the only homemade jam I had eaten, and it tasted better than store-bought jam.

Miss Daisy and her husband did not have children, so I wondered why she baked so much. I know she and her husband could not have eaten all of it. She probably gave most of the sweets she baked to the other children in the neighborhood. I know they must have enjoyed their share just as much as I did mine.

Cle and I saw each other as often as we could. I made up excuses to get away from the house so that we could be together. My best excuse was to get permission to visit Miss Daisy. I would sit and listen to her stories about her life. After I listened for a while, I would tell her I had to leave but would return. She never asked me where I was going or with whom. Although I did not want her to tell Aunt Berenice what I had been doing, I never asked Miss Daisy not to tell her. Miss Daisy was a sweet, older lady who never would have said anything unless she was asked. If asked, however, she would tell the truth. Whenever I was given an opportunity to get away from home, I tried to include Cle. I spent more and more time with him.

Neither Aunt Berenice nor my mother ever gave me reason to think they did not believe my ruse—that my entire time away from home was spent with Miss Daisy when I was supposed to be there. I continued with that deception for months..

One day on my return from the store, while I was handing Aunt Berenice the paper bag, I asked, "Aunt Berenice, can I go to the park for a little while?"

"Yes, but don't be gone too long," was her surprising response.

I rushed out of the house before she could change her mind. That was the only time I had asked her to go to the park, without having to ask permission of my mother. Before I reached the pavilion, I saw Cleveland sitting in his usual spot on top of one of the wooden picnic tables facing my direction. Although I tried, I could not hide my excitement. Aunt Berenice had let me go to the park, and the fact that Cleveland was there was good reason to be excited.

Cleveland's body was more muscular than all the other boys I had seen in school. Whenever other boys were sitting under the pavilion and he sat down, some of the other boys would acknowledge him and then get up and leave. It seemed almost as if they were afraid of him. Those who remained would talk with him about weightlifting and ask questions 1such as how much he bench-pressed. The fact that he lifted weights every day was one thing I learned from listening to them talk. Cleveland's chiseled body was admired by many boys and girls, and he knew it. He enjoyed talking about weight lifting. If the boys were not talking about weight lifting, it was football.

Listening to all their sports talk must have affected me, because on one occasion, without permission, I decided to stay after school and try out for the girls' track team. I was not as fast as some of the others. After tryouts, I was walking home, and out of nowhere Cleveland joined me.

"You were pretty good out there," he said.

"I was not. Most of the girls were faster than me."

"You weren't the worse," he jokingly said.

"Thanks," I replied. We continued to walk. Then I said, "I didn't see you out there."

"I know."

"I'm glad I didn't know you were there."

"Why?"

"Because I would have been nervous, and my time would have been worse."

We continued to walk when a familiar car suddenly pulled to a stop in front of us. It was Uncle John.

"Get in," he demanded.

Neither Cleveland nor I said a word, but I obeyed and got into the car. Once I was inside, Uncle John shouted, "Didn't I tell you to stay away from that boy?"

"Yes, but I was not with him. I stayed after school to try out for the track team."

"Who gave you permission to do that?"

"Nobody."

"Who gave you permission?"

"Nobody!" I shouted back.

"Your aunt Berenice has been worried sick about you, and I have been looking all over for you. You are not allowed to stay after school for anything. Remember that."

As soon as we walked into the house, he shouted in a loud and angry voice, "Do you know who she was with?"

Before Aunt Berenice could respond, he said, "She was with Cle, CH and Gracie's kid. I told her to stay away from him."

He then looked at me and shouted, "Get into the bedroom, and don't come out."

Shortly thereafter, he came into the room holding a thick, black belt and began to whip me. I jumped up on the bed, trying to get away. That was the first time anyone had whipped me. My jumping on the bed did not prevent that belt from reaching me. I screamed and screamed, but he kept swinging that belt.

"This will teach you to not disobey!" he shouted as he swung the belt.

"OK! I won't do it anymore!" I screamed.

"This will teach you to not disobey me and to stay away from that boy! I told you not to hang out with him!"

He just kept swinging that belt, and it was not missing any part of me. It seemed as if he whipped me for a long time. When he finally stopped, I ran into the bathroom. Big, red whelps were all over my legs and arms. Although I could not see the whelps on my back, the pain let me know they were there. Every place that belt had touched hurt and stung like nothing I had ever felt before.

My weeping stopped when I heard Uncle John's voice. "Jo-Ann, come out of that bathroom!"

I slowly opened the bathroom door and tried to tiptoe into Wimpy's bedroom.

"Where do you think you're going?" he asked. Unable to respond, I stood there and whimpered uncontrollably. My voice quivered, and then again I broke out into loud cries.

Unsympathetically he ordered, "Stop that crying, go into the bedroom, and stay there until your mother comes home."

I eased onto the bed on my stomach and closed my eyes. It hurt to lie on my side or my back. Why did I have to move to Florida? At that moment I wished I were still in New York with Uncle Nick. I hated Uncle John for giving me the worst experience of my life and disliked Aunt Berenice because she had not tried to stop him from whipping me. My body hurt every place that had been touched with that belt, and my body was on fire. The nuns had never whipped me. That day I would have welcomed their chastisement. At least when we did something wrong at Sacred Heart, we were punished or chastised but not whipped with a belt. After Uncle John's beating, I was unable to walk upright because of the pain.

From that day on, whenever I was at Aunt Berenice's house and Uncle John walked in, I would leave the room or go next door. It would be quite some time before I even spoke with Uncle John after that incident—and when I did, it was because I had to.

## CHAPTER SEVENTEEN

# YOU DIDN'T RAISE ME!

Finally I had gotten the opportunity to live with my mother. Living with my mother was quite different from living with the Johnsons or Uncle Nick. The atmosphere was tense, and I did not feel comfortable. When I was around her, I seemed to be at a loss for words. This had not been a problem prior to living with her. It was as if a sudden fear came over me when I attempted a simple conversation. I would freeze—nothing would come out of my mouth. I only spoke with my mother for permission to go next door or to the store or to the park. I would ask quickly as I headed toward the front door. If she had ever denied me permission, I would have had to stop in my tracks. My mother only spoke with me to tell me what she wanted done around the house or what Aunt Berenice needed to have done. One Saturday morning after having cleaned my room, I was on my way to the kitchen when I saw my mother at the kitchen table drinking a cup of coffee and smoking a cigarette. I said, "When I finish cleaning the kitchen, I am going over to Aunt Berenice's house."

The sudden pull on my arm not only surprised me but stopped me in my tracks.

"You need to spend more time at home!" she said in a very agitated tone. "You are at Aunt Berenice's house every day and don't spend enough time here."

"You told me that you wanted me to go to her house to help her out. Aunt Berenice always has something for me to do over there."

"She doesn't need you every minute! I noticed that you call her Aunt Berenice, but you don't call me Mother. I'm your mother, and from now on, that's what I expect to be called."

I pulled my arm away from her.

"You can't force me to call you that. You didn't raise me!" I shouted and walked out of the house.

I hesitated for a moment and then decided against going to Aunt Berenice's house. All I heard was, "Get back in this house!" I ran and did not stop until I reached the park.

My mother never asked me about my life at Sacred Heart or life with the Johnsons. I could not figure out if she was just not interested or was afraid to bring up the subject. She did not talk about it, nor did I. While I lived at Sacred Heart, I wished I had been living with her instead. Life with my mother was nothing like I imagined. When she looked at me, it was with no special enthusiasm. We were complete strangers to each other. The discomfort between us was palpable and mutual. It was as if my life shut down when I was in the house. There were many questions I would have liked answered but was afraid to ask, such as: Why didn't you ever try to get in touch with me? Did you know I lived in a foster home? Why did you never write to me? I do not even know if I would have liked the answers to those questions, and maybe that is why I did not ask them. Also if those questions were asked and answered, would they have made a difference in our relationship? I will never know. Pondering these questions made my life feel empty.

If she were sitting in the living room and I entered, she would go outside to the front porch. If I were sitting in the living room and she entered, I would get up and go into my bedroom or to the front porch, or I would ask permission to go to Aunt Berenice's house. I do not know why we avoided each other's company. We communicated only when it was absolutely necessary.

The two and one-half years I lived with my mother were a relatively short segment of my life. I should have made an effort to get to know her as a person and learn as much as I could about her, but my internal pain, heartache, and, I believe, pride prevented me from reaching out to her. That time we spent together should have been an eternity, but in reality, it was a brief moment that neither of us used to our advantage.

As a child, I blamed myself for being the reason my mother left me at that place. I thought she had given me away because she did not want me. Also I created imaginary reasons for my being under the care and responsibility of the nuns at Sacred Heart Orphanage Asylum. I thought they took care of girls who did not have parents or who were not wanted by their parents or who had run away from home or any number of reasons; however, I never imagined that girls could have been at that home because they had behavior or mental problems, as the word asylum might imply. If they had those problems, I was too young to know or recognize them.

Reflecting on my relationship with my mother reminded me of my relationship with the nuns who raised me. I had later learned to be less afraid of the nuns to the point where I had begun to talk back and manipulate circumstances to my advantage. Now I was defying my mother.

## CHAPTER EIGHTEEN

# RUNAWAY

When I ran away from my mother to the park, I sat at one of the tables under the pavilion where several children and adults were laughing and talking. After I listened for a few minutes to their chatter, a familiar voice said, "Hey! What are you doing up here?"

I turned and saw Lawrence with a big smile on his face.

"I came up here to get away from the house for a while," I said.

"I haven't seen you at the park before."

"I have not seen you here, either."

Lawrence sat next to me and added, "I'm surprised you're not reading a book."

"I do other things besides read," I replied.

"I would like to find out what some of those other things are," a familiar voice said.

When I turned in the direction of that voice, I saw Cleveland. He smiled and sat at the opposite side of the table.

"Hey, Cle," Lawrence said.

"Hey, what's up, man?" said Cleveland.

"Not much."

Cleveland looked at me and said, "Hi, Red."

With squinted eyes, I asked, "Are you talking to me?"

In all the time we spent together, he had never called me anything but my name.

"Yeah," he said.

In a raised voice, I responded, "My name is Jo-Ann, as if you didn't know!"

"From now on, I am going to call you Red. That is a good nickname for you."

"I do not need or want a nickname. Why do most of the people who live down here have nicknames anyway?"

Cle did not answer and looked at Lawrence. Lawrence said, "Maybe it's because if two people have the same first name, it's easier to know which person we're talking to or about." He laughed. "I really don't know."

"Since I have been living here, I have not met two people with the same first name," I said.

Lawrence said, "Look, I really don't know why a lot of people have nicknames. I was just trying to come up with something that made sense."

Cleveland winked at Lawrence. "What you said makes sense to me."

"Lawrence, what's your nickname?" I asked.

"I don't have one."

Trying to be cool, I said, "I bet I could make up a good one for you."

"Yeah? Like what?"

"Well, um, um…Slim is a good one."

Lawrence said. "You're kidding. There's a guy around here who already has that nickname."

"Well, we definitely would not want two people to have the same nickname," I said.

"Why did you say Slim?"

"Because you are tall and slim, that's a good nickname for you."

Lawrence responded, "Too bad someone else already has it."

"Well, I'll just have to think of another one for you."

"Lawrence, what do you think about the nickname I gave her?" Cleveland asked.

Lawrence hunched his shoulders, "I don't know."

"Well, I don't like it," I said.

"Red, I've got to go, but I'll see you around," Lawrence said. Then he laughed and walked away.

"Lawrence, don't leave!" I said. "I have not decided on a nickname for you yet."

He turned toward me and said, "You will probably have a nickname for me the next time I see you."

I wished Lawrence had stayed, because there was so much we could have talked about. He was not only cute but smart—and a nice guy. I continued to watch him until he faded in the distance.

Cle was dressed in his usual tight T-shirt and Levi's.

"What are you doing at the park today?" he asked.

"My mother and I had an argument, so I ran out of the house and ended up here," I said

"And she didn't come after you?"

"Nope."

"I've got to go to the store," Cle said. "Do you want to walk with me?"

"No."

"Oh, come on. It's a short walk. We'll come right back."

I looked behind me several times as we walked to the store. Cleveland spoke about going to college, playing professional football, and moving away from Florida someday.

On our way back from the store, he said, "I have to take this to my mother. Do you want to walk to my house with me?"

"Where do you live?"

"Right over there." He pointed to a house across the street from the other side of the park.

"OK, but I cannot stay long."

When we reached his front yard, I noticed a bench and barbells on the ground. A guy walking by yelled, "Hey, Cle, are you going to lift weights today?"

"Later."

We reached his house to find his parents sitting on the porch.

Cle said, "Mom, Dad, this is Red…I mean Jo-Ann." He looked at me and smiled.

"Hello," I said.

"Hey, child," replied his mother.

His father nodded his head in acknowledgment, as he was busy sprinkling tobacco from a red Prince Albert can onto a white piece of paper. He rolled the paper around the tobacco and then licked the edge of it, never looking away from his cigarette. His mother was robust and very dark in complexion with neatly braided hair. Her face was written with hard work and tired eyes, but her pearly white teeth shone through with her smile. Her bare feet were ashen and cracked.

His father looked much taller than his mother. He had thick eyebrows and kind eyes, and his strongly chiseled face exuded life. He was wearing a short-sleeved T-shirt under his overalls and sat with his legs crossed—making it possible for me to notice his dust-covered shoes. Cleveland's father was the more handsome of his parents

Cleveland had the same thick eyebrows and chiseled facial features as his father. "We're going back to the park," Cleveland said.

His mother abruptly added with an accent I had not heard before, "Cle, can't you'al sit down for a few minutes?"

Cleveland looked at me, and I nodded yes.

His mother looked me over from head to toe. "Who are your kinfolks?" she asked.

"My mother's name is Ruthine Cave."

"I never heard of her. Who's she kin to?"

"My mother has a sister who lives here with her husband."

"What's her name?" Cleveland's father asked.

"Berenice Minnis."

"There's a lot of Minnises in this town, but I never heard of her," his mother said.

"She's married to John Minnis," I said.

"Oh, we know John," Cle's father said.

"Ain't he married to a high-yella woman?" his mother asked.

Her way with words was different from anything I had heard before. I had never heard anyone describe another person in those words, but I responded, "Yes. She's my aunt Berenice."

They asked me about some of Uncle John's relatives about whom I knew nothing. Cleveland noticed my discomfort from being asked all those questions and said, "Mom, Pop, Jo-Ann has to go now. I'll bring her back some other time."

As we were leaving his home, I again noticed the barbells on the ground. He was truly a weight lifter. "Do you lift weights every day?" I asked.

"Yeah, that's how I keep in shape."

"They look very heavy."

"No. They're only heavy if I put too much weight on the bar."

"I never saw any body lift weights before. Does it hurt?"

He looked at me and laughed.

"Do you want to see me lift some?" he asked.

"Sure," I said.

"Usually when I lift weights, I take my shirt off."

In a cheerful voice, I retorted, "Keep your shirt on."

I watched him adjust the weights and begin to lift them. As soon as some boys noticed him, they stopped to watch. Cleveland lifted weights for a few minutes and then stopped—probably because of the scorching sun. In that short period of time, sweat soaked through his shirt, and he looked as if his body would burst from his shirt as well.

"I can see why you do that with your shirt off," I said.

One of the onlookers asked, "How much did you bench-press this time?"

Cleveland did not respond to him, but he reached for my hand and said, "Come on, Jo-Ann. I'd better get you back to the park before your folks find out you are over here."

During our walk back to the park, I asked, "Where is your mother from? I never heard anyone speak with that accent before."

"My mother was born in Nassau."

"Where's Nassau?"

"In the Bahamas."

"That's where my uncle John was born, but he doesn't have a sharp accent like your mother."

Many of the Nassau-born people in that town knew each other. I later learned that many Bahamian people lived in Florida. We walked through the park and sat under the pavilion.

Dusk had crept up on us before I realized how long I had been away from home. I kept looking in the direction of our apartment for a familiar face or a voice demanding me to return home. Although I did not want to return home with my mother, I did wish someone would come for me. The thought that my mother probably did not want me to live with her persisted. This was not the first time I thought that way. To my surprise, Uncle John did not even show up. Maybe she had not told him and Aunt Berenice what happened between us, or maybe she was waiting for me to return on my own.

People sporadically left the pavilion until the only two people left were Cleveland and me. "Don't you think you should go home now?" he said.

"No, I don't want to go back there."

"You can't stay in the park all night," he said.

When I heard those words, I was suddenly frightened. I had not even felt as frightened when I ran away from Sacred Heart.

"Who else can you spend the night with?" he asked.

"No one. I do not have any other relatives here or any friends I can stay with tonight." In a low quivering voice, I added, "I never wanted to come down here to live anyway. I wish I could have stayed in New York with my uncle. I hate living down here!"

He quickly switched the conversation. "Let's go for a walk. It might take your mind off things."

I walked farther that evening than the whole time I had been in Florida, past blocks of buildings that were all different: homes, apartments, some churches, barbershops, the American Legion bar where Uncle John worked, and three neighborhood grocery stores. One interesting thing about our walk was that most of it was not on sidewalks but on the streets. As many times as I had walked to the store for Aunt Berenice, I didn't realize that other neighborhoods also did not have sidewalks.

To my amazement, the most interesting thing I noticed during our walk was that, of the many people we saw, none were white.

"Aren't there any white people who live around here?" I asked.

"There are lots of white people who live in this town but on the other side of the railroad tracks."

"Why do they live on the other side of the railroad tracks?"

"This is the south. Many white folks down here are prejudiced and prefer to live separately from black people. In many towns in the south, whites live on one side of the railroad tracks and blacks on the other."

Once we crossed the railroad tracks, there were sidewalks on every street, and I saw white people in every direction. We walked for several more blocks before I decided it was time to go back. Upon our arrival at the park, I glanced down the street in the direction of my house. I didn't see anyone or anything peculiar. To my amazement, there were many people sitting under the pavilion. "Are you ready to go back home?" Cle asked. "No. My mother doesn't care where I am." I replied. There was no place for us to sit. Cle took my hand and said, "Come on. Let's walk and talk some more."

## CHAPTER NINETEEN

# OH, WHAT A NIGHT!

That night, Cle and I continued our walk arriving at a large, empty parcel of land. Cleveland took my hand and guided me to an area he thought best.

"Let's sit down here," he said.

The evening was full of warmth with a clear sky that allowed the textured blanket of grass to glimmer in the moonlight. We sat on the grass facing each other.

"Have you ever had a boyfriend?" he asked.

At that moment I did not want to seem immature, so I hastily replied, "Of course, when I lived in New York." As soon as those words left my mouth, I regretted having said them.

"So you kissed a boy before?"

"Of course I did," I lied.

He pulled my shoulders toward him and kissed my lips. *What have I gotten myself into*, I thought and pulled away. He tried to kiss me again, but that time I pushed him away and said, "Don't do that!"

"What's the matter?"

"Just because I said I had a boyfriend and had been kissed by a boy does not mean I want you to kiss me. You are not my boyfriend."

Cleveland reached for my hand as he said, "No, I am not your boyfriend, but I would like to be."

He said, "I really enjoy spending time with you, Jo-Ann. You're not like the other girls I know. You are more interesting. I like talking with you."

I said, "You know, I also enjoy spending time with you—and I like the fact that you listen to me." I lowered my gaze and said, "I really didn't have a boyfriend when I lived in New York. There was a boy I liked, but we weren't boyfriend and girlfriend. It was more of a crush on my part than anything."

I was nervous and speechless. I could not believe that he wanted to be my boyfriend.

He reached for my hand and asked, "Are you going to give me an answer?"

I sat in thoughtful silence, deciding whether to accept his offer. I thought about what my mother would say. I already knew what Uncle John's response would be, and Aunt Berenice would agree with him. I said, "I have to think about it."

"Good."

Cle placed his arm around my shoulders, and this time I didn't pull away. A peaceful, calming feeling embraced me. We sat speechless for a short time, and then he kissed my lips. Prior to that moment, I had never been kissed that way by a boy. And when he kissed me again, I responded favorably. My mind and body seemed to be racing against each other. My thinking was scrambled while my body tingled. I didn't understand what was happening to me, but I enjoyed it and wanted those feelings to continue. When I felt his hand on my arm, it was a very soft, delicate touch, hardly the touch of someone with a rugged, well-chiseled weight lifter's body.

He held my head against his chest and lay back onto the ground. His chest was firm and felt better than any pillow I had ever laid my head upon. I moved my hands over his broad shoulders, and his hands tightened around my waist. We kissed and hugged each other, and Cle's hands moved slowly, exploring other areas of my body. I was nervous, but he was gentle—which enabled me to relax. We made love.

That night I traveled through a different sphere where I saw stars and had mixed feelings of seismic proportions. Afterward I lay with my head on his chest for what seemed like an eternity. I wanted to get up, but my mind and body wouldn't let me.

Finally I arose from his chest, stared expressionlessly at him, and said, "We should go back to the park. It is getting late."

"You can't stay in the park all night. Why don't you let me walk you home?"

"No. I am not going back to that house!"

"Then why don't you come home with me?"

"That is not a good idea."

"You can sleep in my room."

"That is even worse. Your parents will not let me sleep in their house—and surely not in your room."

"I will not tell them. They won't even know you are there. We can go in through the back, because my bedroom is in the back of the house."

149

My eyes widened, and my voice seemed to get louder when I said, "You must be crazy! I am not going to sleep in your house or in your room or in your bed!"

"I am not crazy. I just want to help you out. You can sleep in my bed, and I will sleep on the floor. No one will ever know."

"Your parents might see me."

"No, they won't."

"Why would you do that for me?"

"I like you and do not want you to spend the night outside." He took my hand and pulled me up from the grass. "Come on, let's go."

I quietly followed Cle to the back of his home, and we slipped through the door into his bedroom. The room was totally dark. There was only silence in the home. When he turned on the light, I could see that his room was spotless. I was amazed at how well his bed was made. It did not have a bedspread on it, but the sheets were pulled so tight that there were no wrinkles to be seen. The nuns would have liked the way his bed was made.

"Why don't you sit down?" he said in a low voice. He saw me gazing around the room for a chair and said, "You can sit on the bed. The bathroom is outside that door we just came through and on the right."

The sheets were pulled so tight that I thought they would snap if I sat on them. Slowly I eased myself down onto the bed with my hands resting at its edge.

"If you are tired," he said, "go ahead and lie down." His soft-spoken voice gave me a sense of security, but I still felt uncomfortable being in his home and bedroom. "I won't touch you," he said.

I did not speak for fear of being heard by his parents. Sitting upright without anything to lean my back against was tiresome, so

I decided to lie down. I listened for sounds of his parents stirring or walking around—but there wasn't a sound.

"What if your parents come back here?" I whispered.

He said, "They won't come back here tonight, but they do get up early in the morning. We will be gone by then."

I slipped out of my flip-flops and lay on top of the sheets. "You can lie between the sheets," he laughed. He put a blanket on the floor next to the bed with a sheet on top and lay down. I felt bad that I enjoyed the comfort of his bed while he was on the floor.

While I lay there, I thought about what had transpired between my mother and me earlier that day—and what had led up to that interaction. So many thoughts ran through my mind. Also I worried that his parents would walk through the door at any minute and find me—not only in their home but in their son's bed. Before that night, I had never slept in another person's bed. I could not risk falling asleep and having his parents find me in their son's bed. Every sound I heard gave me reason to fidget nervously. My eyes were heavy, but I was much too afraid to let sleep overcome me.

I do believe I slept early the next morning, because while it was still dark outside, I heard Cle say, "We'd better get ready to go now. My parents will be up soon."

I felt as if I had just fallen asleep and did not want to get up—but I knew I had to. I did not see a clock in his room and wondered how he knew when his parents would get up or if he knew the time. While I straightened the sheets, I heard a door open and turned in its direction.

"Where are you going?" I whispered.

"I'm going to the bathroom!"

"Don't leave me in here by myself."

"OK," he said and closed the door.

The sheets did not look as straight as they previously had, but the bed was made up. We left the room together. As we approached the bathroom door, he said, "You go in first. I will wait here." He stood outside the door as I closed it. When I came out, he went in.

The entire time I stood there—which was only for a few minutes—I was nervous, imagining his mother or father finding me in their home. When I saw that bathroom door open, I breathed a sigh of relief. Once we were outside the house, he said, "Wait here. I want to make sure my parents are not sitting on the porch. They usually get up early and sit on the porch to drink their coffee."

As the backyard was fenced, we could not leave that way, but there was no fence on the right side of the house. Perhaps that would be our means of escape. Cle returned and took my hand.

"They are not up yet. Let's go," he said.

He walked in his regular manner, while I tried to tiptoe to prevent sound escaping from under my footsteps.

The streets were quiet and empty. By the time we reached the park, I saw a few cars drive by. The only way people could see us was if they walked right up to the park or if car lights shone in our direction.

I leaned closer to Cle and whispered, "What do you think my mother will do if I go back home?"

"Jo-Ann, why are you whispering? No one is going to hear you."

I looked in all directions. "You would think someone would be walking the streets by now. What time do you think it is?" I asked.

"I don't know. But the lights are on in my parents' house, so it must be around four o'clock."

"Do your parents get up this early every morning?"

"Yeah, they're farmers who are out in the fields by the time the sun rises."

I looked toward his parents' home, which stood out among the other dark houses on that block. I was glad the pavilion did not have lights—so we could not be seen.

"A good sign for you this morning is that the police are not riding around here," he said.

"What does that mean?" I asked.

"I guess your mother did not call the police, because if she had, they probably would be around the area looking for you."

"Why would she call the police when all she has to do is tell Uncle John? I don't think the police would whip me the way he did."

I sat in the park and waited for my mother or Uncle John to come looking for me, but neither did.

"Jo-Ann, you can't stay in the park all day," Cleveland said. "You should go home."

"What for?" I asked. "My mother does not want me, and I do not want to live with her, either."

"You are upset right now. Maybe she thinks you will not go with her if she comes for you, or maybe she looked for you last night. Or perhaps she is walking around looking for you now. I bet she is just as upset as you are."

"She is probably upset because I am living with her—not because I did not return home last night."

"That's not true. Come on, let me walk you home."

When he asked to walk me home knowing how my family felt about him, it made me care for him even more.

"No. I cannot be seen with you. The last time I was seen with you, my uncle beat me with a thick, black belt, and I was sore all over. I don't know what he is going to do this time, but if he whips me like that again, I am going to run away for good."

"They will probably be so glad to see that you are OK, they won't even think about whipping you. Go home. I will wait here for a while in case you come back."

"You will do that for me?"

"Of course I will."

We finally agreed that I should go home.

"Thanks for your help last night. I don't know what I would have done without you," I said.

"You don't have to thank me. I would do it again."

I walked across the street, looked back, and waved.

## CHAPTER TWENTY

# RAPE

My heart beat faster with each step that took me closer to the house. Dreaded consequences of my actions overwhelmed my mind. I decided not to knock on Aunt Berenice and Uncle John's door, because my uncle would probably be waiting for me with a belt in his hands. When I approached Aunt Berenice's house, I walked slowly, and during that time, I thought slow meant quiet. The windows on her front door were open. Did she see me but not say anything? When I reached my mother's front door, I turned the knob, but the door did not open. So I knocked. My mother did not answer, so I knocked louder the second time.

"Who is it?" I heard.

At that point my voice trembled. "Me," I replied.

"Who is me?"

She knew my voice and had to know who was at the door. I really did not want to be there and believed she did not want me there. As I turned toward the steps to leave, I heard the door being unlocked.

"It's about time you decided to come home," she said.

I looked at her intensely and tried to pierce the blank expression on her face to discover what thoughts and feelings were hidden behind it. She was wearing the same clothes she had worn the day before, now wrinkled on her small frame. I stood motionless until she gestured with cigarette in hand.

"Get in here right now," she said.

My eyes widened at the tone of her voice. Before she could say another word, I walked past her and sat on the couch. My mother sat in the chair, grinding out her cigarette in the ashtray. She drew a deep, unsteady sigh.

"Where were you last night?"

I paused for a moment before deciding what to say. "I was at the park," I responded in a trembling voice.

"You mean to tell me you spent the entire night at the park?"

Shifting uncertainly on the couch with my hands clenched, I simply glanced in her direction and replied, "Yes."

"Your uncle John and I walked through the park several times last night, but we did not see you."

I shrugged. "I probably was not there when you and Uncle John were there," I said sarcastically before I realized how my response must have sounded.

She hesitated and glanced at me with a squint-eyed expression. "Don't lie to me, young lady. If you were not at the park, where were you?"

At that moment I felt a fleeting sense of uneasiness. Was it guilt? Could she see it on my face? I did not know. It could have been a sudden, overwhelming sense of guilt. One thing was certain; I did not want to tell her exactly where and with whom I was. With a steady gaze and voice, I said, "I was walking around with some school friends. We walked around here and then uptown."

Silence engulfed the room until she asked, "And?"

"And when we returned from our walk, the other kids went home, and I went to the park."

"Was anyone else with you at the park?" she asked.

"Yes."

"Who?"

"Cle."

"Who?"

"Cleveland Barrett."

"Isn't he the boy your uncle told you to stay away from?"

"Yes."

"And what were you doing with him?"

"We were talking."

"Where were you talking? It wasn't in the park. We walked around the park several times, and you weren't there. Where were you?"

My hands were shaking. I placed them between my knees, but that didn't help. Tears rolled down my cheeks. My legs were bobbing up and down.

"I asked you a question!" she said sharply.

"I don't know."

"You don't know where you walked?" she asked in a raised voice.

"No—No—I don't know."

My mother momentarily hesitated and then burst out, "Did you have sex with that boy?"

I sat stunned for a minute, unable to look at her. In a low voice with tears streaming down my cheeks, I answered, "Yes."

"What? What have you done?"

Her horrified expression frightened me, and all I could do was weep.

"I was up all night worried about you, and you were out having sex with that boy!" She stormed out and went next door. Upon her return, she shouted, "Go over to your aunt Berenice's house!"

When I heard those words, the first thing that came to mind was to run away, but I resisted that urge and went to Aunt Berenice's house.

In a steady and calm voice, Aunt Berenice said, "Jo-Ann, tell me what happened last night."

The words spilled out as I continued to weep. "Cle and I went for a walk last night and ended up in a field or empty lot, where we had sex."

"Have you ever had sex before?"

"No."

Aunt Berenice's calmness made me feel at ease until she abruptly stated, "I'm calling the police. He raped her!"

The police were called and came to Aunt Berenice's house. Upon their arrival, Aunt Berenice immediately told them I had been raped. They asked me questions. One officer said, "Take your time."

After he said that, I began to relax. My mother interrupted with her own questions.

One policeman seemed agitated and said, "Ma'am, we'll ask the questions."

I repeated what I had told my mother and aunt. However, when asked why I didn't come home, I hesitated and said, "Ah…I didn't think my mother wanted me home."

Startled, she looked at me and asked before the police could ask another question, "Did you sleep in the park?"

"Ma'am…"

Before he could finish, I said slowly, "Well, I lay on the picnic table bench under the pavilion, but I did not go to sleep."

She moistened her lips, frowned, and blinked with an I-don't-believe-you look on her face. "Did he stay at the park with you?" she asked.

Nervously fidgeting and loudly crying, I responded, "Yes!"

The police spoke with my mother and aunt for a short period and left.

My mother shouted, "Go home, take a bath, and change your clothes. When you finish, straighten up your bedroom, the living room, and clean the kitchen."

My room was already straightened up, but I did not say anything. I was surprised but happy that Uncle John wasn't home. Without hesitation, I rushed to the bathroom and turned on the water in the bathtub. That day I stayed in the tub longer than usual, thinking about all that had happened the day before. Once I finished bathing, I opened the door a crack and placed my ear against the small opening. There was silence throughout the house. I quietly walked to my bedroom.

Suddenly I felt hungry—but too afraid to go into the kitchen to prepare something to eat. Yesterday I did not think about food. Now I desperately wanted anything to rid me of the hunger. The more I thought about food, the hungrier I became. *Maybe I should wait until*

*I clean the kitchen before I prepare a bowl of cornflakes*, I thought. At that moment I decided the kitchen would be cleaned first.

Several days later when Aunt Berenice and my mother were sitting on the porch, I heard my aunt tell my mother that Cle had been arrested for rape. I didn't know what that meant, but the next time I was at Aunt Berenice's house, I asked, "Why was Cle arrested?"

She explained that he had sex with me and I was an underage girl. Cle was nineteen, and I was fifteen.

"That's called rape," she said. "Cle's been arrested for raping you."

I was shocked and unable to speak. The information I had given the police resulted in Cle being arrested. How could this have happened?

I don't know how long after the police were at the house that Aunt Berenice shocked me yet again. "Jo-Ann, next month you'll have to go to court to testify about what Cle did to you."

My stomach tightened. I was speechless. She went on for several minutes, explaining the long, drawn-out process. After hearing her, there was no way that I was going to utter a word. Although I didn't say anything, I felt terrible about the whole situation.

When that day came, I felt so guilty that I was unable to look at Cleveland's face. How had we wound up here? It was my fault, but I didn't know how to fix it. An attorney started by talking to me, but I don't remember what he said. His words sounded as if they echoed through a tunnel. I heard him, but it was difficult for me to grasp what was being said. When I began to cry, he stopped talking, and I felt relieved. That did not last long.

The first question I remember him asking after his silence was, "Did you sneak out of your house one night in your pajamas to meet Cleveland Barrett?"

*That's a stupid question. Why would he ask me that question?* I thought. But I sarcastically responded, "No. I don't wear pajamas."

More than anything, I wanted to run out of that courtroom and not return. The next question he asked was, "Had you previously had sex with Cleveland Barrett?"

I sat quietly looking down at my hands.

"A simple yes or no."

Suddenly I got the strength to look directly into Cle's eyes and said, "Yes."

A gush of sighs permeated the courtroom. We looked at each other, and neither of us blinked.

"Will you repeat your answer?" the attorney replied.

Still looking in Cle's direction, I blurted, "Yes!"

"Yes, what?" he asked.

Still staring at Cle, with a raised voice, I said, "Yes, I did have sex with Cleveland before that night."

The attorney then asked how many times I had sex with Cle. My response was, "I don't know."

He walked closer to me. "You don't know?" he asked.

In a more composed state, I answered, "I don't remember."

"You don't remember how many times you and Cleveland Barrett had sex?"

I hesitated before saying, "Two or three."

"You had sex with Cleveland Barrett two or three times?"

"Yes."

On our way home from court, my mother and I didn't speak. The minute we walked through the front door, she shouted, "How dare you lie and embarrass me! You embarrassed the whole family."

"I didn't lie," I said. "You and Aunt Berenice are the ones who called the police—not me."

We screamed at each other. I hurried to my bedroom and slammed the door. It was opened just as quickly as my mother yelled, "As long as you live in my house, don't ever slam another door!"

I flopped onto my bed when I realized I really didn't want to respond to her. She walked away, but her cigarette smoke drifted into my room. A short time later, I heard the front door slam. I stared at the ceiling with disbelief of what had occurred earlier and put my pillow over my head, hoping to block out the entire event.

The rest of that day was a blur—until I learned Cleveland was found not guilty. I was happy and relieved because of the not-guilty verdict but sad because of the trouble I had caused him.

## CHAPTER TWENTY-ONE

# APOLOGY

Cle experienced arrest, a rape charge, and court appearance all because of me. I wanted and needed to talk with him now more than ever. I thought he probably would never see or speak with me again. The more I thought about him, the more miserable I felt. Would he accept my apology? What about his parents? What reason would I give them for what I had done?

Before the so-called rape, when I was allowed to go to the park and Cle was not there, I would go to his house and watch him and his friends weightlifting. When I was with him, I did not want to go home. He would always say, "Jo-Ann, don't you think it's time to go home?"

My reply would be, "I really don't want to go home."

"I don't want your uncle John coming to look for me. And if you don't go home, you won't be able to come back tomorrow." That statement was always my decision-maker.

After the whole rape incident, I wasn't allowed to return to the park. My way around that was to visit Miss Daisy's house, leave there, and then go to the park. Sometimes I'd sit at the park for up to an hour hoping to see Cle. I would ask some of the boys on the park if they had seen him. Other times I'd give them messages for him. Whenever I went to the store or ran errands for Aunt Berenice and passed the park, I hoped to see Cle. I had not seen him for weeks. I missed talking with him. He was someone I was able to tell true stories. He listened to me as intently as did those girls at Sacred Heart. He laughed at some of the things I told him about my life at Sacred Heart and seemed truly saddened by others. He asked many questions. We spoke about some of the books I had read and the way I practically lived in and for books. I felt sad when he told me that the only books he read were schoolbooks. But the more we laughed and talked, the more I enjoyed being with him. My times spent with him were the most enjoyable.

One day while at the park, I heard a familiar voice behind me. "Hey, Red."

Startled, I turned to see Cle behind me. One look at him revealed tired, sad eyes that made me regret the pain I caused him. The times I had waited to see Cle seemed like an eternity. Now he was in front of me, and suddenly I was speechless. I opened my mouth to speak, but nothing came out. My vocal cords seemed paralyzed. Somehow I garnered enough strength to stand up, walk toward him, and wrap my arms around his waist. I held on to him so tightly that I couldn't have been pried away.

In a calm, steady voice, he took my hand and said, "Sit down, Red. Let's talk.

My first instinct the moment we sat down was to pour out everything I had held in for weeks. "I'm sorry! I'm sorry for all the trouble and pain I've caused you and your family. Please forgive me. What must your parents think of me? Will they forgive me? Will you ever be able to forgive me? I...I..."

Still holding my hand, he replied, "I forgive you. But most of all, I thank you."

Somewhat bewildered, I asked, "Why on Earth would you thank me?"

"Because you and I know we didn't have sex before. Why did you say we previously had sex?"

I was happy to see a soulful sparkle in his eyes when he asked that question. That look in his eyes caused me to smile and shrug my shoulders. "It was my fault that all of those awful things happened to you. I got you into that mess and didn't know how to fix it. When I looked into your eyes from the witness stand, those words just flowed from my mouth."

"How did your family react to your testimony?" he asked.

"Well, my mother said I embarrassed her—among other things—but I don't care."

"You amaze me, Jo-Ann. I always knew you were special."

"There's nothing special about me," I said with a nervous smile. Then I said, "Cle, I have to get back to Miss Daisy's house."

"Well, in that case," Cle said, glancing down at our hands, "I had better let you go."

I looked up at him and said, "Before I leave, uh...Do you think maybe tomorrow you can take me to see your parents?"

"Sure."

"Should I be worried?" I asked.

"No. They're upset about the whole situation. My mother is very demonstrative. When she's upset or angry she definitely shows it and says whatever is on her mind."

Suddenly I regretted asking Cle to take me to his home. The thoughts persisted that his parents hated me and would never allow me back into their home.

"Maybe I shouldn't go there tomorrow," I said.

"Look, Red, it will be fine. My mother will say what she wants to say, and all you have to do is listen unless she asks you a question. You don't have to worry. I'll be with you."

"OK. I'll see you tomorrow."

For me, Cle's acceptance of my apology lifted a huge weight from my shoulders. But I still wondered how he could be so forgiving. That evening was the first time I truly relaxed and, for a long time, slept the entire night.

The next day Miss Daisy was again my excuse to get away from the house. Cle was waiting for me when I got to the park. I was nervous but happy to see him. Yesterday had been a day of strong emotions. We spent the next few minutes on a lighter note with small talk, but I interrupted with, "Cle, I want to apologize again…uh…"

"Red, you don't have to keep apologizing. I told my parents about our talk yesterday. They definitely want to talk with you."

Hearing those words made me uncomfortable; but I knew that talking with his parents was something I had to do.

"Come on, Red, let's go."

We walked into the house, and I stood tense, not certain if I should sit, until Mr. Barrett motioned me to a seat. I sat down slowly.

The aroma from the kitchen saturated the room. Suddenly I wanted to eat whatever Mrs. Barrett was cooking. How could I possibly think about eating at a time like this?

Cle walked into the kitchen, and a couple minutes later his mother appeared. I looked directly into her face and then lowered my eyes in shame.

"Mr. and Mrs. Barrett," I said, my voice cracking, "I came here to apologize...to say I'm sorry for the trouble I caused you and your son. You deserve not only my apology but also an explanation. Um... when my aunt learned that Cle and I had sex, she called the police. I was scared. They asked me a lot of questions, and I answered them the best I could."

Before I could say another word, Mrs. Barrett's eyes widened, and in a raised voice, she said, "I knew John Minnis had something to do with this. It's his fault."

"No, Mrs. Barrett, it's not like that," I protested. "Uncle John wasn't even home. His wife called the police."

My eyes welled, and I blinked back tears. This was another day of strong emotions. I was more nervous apologizing to Cle's parents than I had been apologizing to him. I folded my hands on my lap and looked at Cle's father, who sat quietly but listened intently, smoking his cigarette.

"Child, we appreciate you coming over here to apologize, but John Minnis and his wife should be here, not you," Mrs. Barrett said. Her husband nodded his head in agreement.

"Jo-Ann, all of us are to blame," Cle said, "including your aunt and mother. All of us contributed to this awful situation. My life has been turned upside down, and I can't imagine what all of this is doing to you."

I was amazed at how understanding Cle was after all that had happened to him. His attitude about the entire situation made me care for him even more.

"Cle, what I've gone through can't in any way be compared to the terrible things you experienced," I said.

He reached for my hand, but I nervously pulled back. What must his parents think? Cle sensed my nervousness.

"Red, I think it's time for you to go home," he said.

I stood up and instinctively made my way to where Mrs. Barrett sat, and I hugged her. "I'm so sorry. I'm sorry for everything," I said.

She did not return my hug but said, "Child, it's in God's hands. He took care of it then and is still taking care of it now."

Hearing those words brought on my tears. I walked over to Mr. Barrett and put out my hand, which he accepted, but he never uttered a word.

"Mr. Barrett, I'm sorry."

Cle took my hand, and this time I did not pull away.

"Come on, Red. We'd better go."

I left Cleveland's home feeling very sad.

I couldn't stop thinking about what had taken place—even after I returned home. I wondered what his parents thought of me. They did not verbally forgive me, but they did not turn me away from their home, either. I could not understand why Mr. Barrett was so quiet. Cleveland seemed to have more traits of his father than his mother.

That night I lay in bed with various thoughts streaming through my mind. The demeanor of Cle's parents when I was at their home earlier was new to me. And, the fact that they allowed me into their home after all that had happened was astonishing. I had not visited or spoken with them since the day we first met. Mrs. Barrett had done all the talking in a sometimes elevated voice. She did not berate me or use abusive language. Although her husband appeared composed, when I looked into his eyes I saw the pain. I wondered if his look of sadness would ever dissipate. I wondered if Cle's parents would ever forgive me.

Cle was very much on my mind as well. When we were not together, I wanted to see him—even if just for a glimpse as I walked by the park.

## CHAPTER TWENTY-TWO

# SHE CAN'T EVEN BOIL WATER

My anticipation of Cleveland's reaction to the news of me being pregnant was nerve-racking.

I stared into Cleveland's eyes as we sat on the park bench. "Cle, I have something important to tell you."

"What is it?"

I swallowed and then said, "I am pregnant, and I do not know how I am going to tell my mother."

"Are you sure?" he asked.

A tear dropped into my lap, and I twisted my hands nervously. "Yes. I am sure. I'm several months late. What should I do?"

I probably had a look of apprehension and uncertainty when he took my hand.

"Relax. Don't worry. I'll go talk with your mother."

In response, I sighed softly and said, "That will not do any good. She did not even want me to spend time or be seen with you. What do you think she will say about this?"

He gazed at me with silent curiosity and held my hand a little tighter. I felt myself relaxing.

"She probably will not let you inside the house." I said.

"If she does, let me do the talking. I don't know what I am going to say until I am there and start talking." That seemed to be a strange statement, due to the circumstances.

"You should know what you are going to say before you go there."

"Listen, I will tell her you are pregnant and ask if I can marry you."

"What? Get married? She has never met you. My mother will never agree to that."

"Jo-Ann, it will not hurt to try. What else can we do?"

"We can run away," I said.

"Jo-Ann, running away is not the solution to everything."

"Let's not tell her today, maybe in a couple of days. I am not ready."

When we decided it was time to inform my mother, Cle came to my house. He looked so strong and unafraid, but I was nervous the moment he walked through the door.

"Good evening Miss Cave," he said. "My name is Cleveland Barrett."

"Hello. I have heard about you," she replied but did not offer him a seat. He stood in the doorway.

"Why don't you sit down?" I said. He came to sit next to me on the couch.

"Miss Cave, Jo-Ann is pregnant, and I am here to ask your permission to marry her."

"What? Are you the boy Jo-Ann's uncle said he did not want her to associate with?"

Cleveland looked at me, and before he could respond, I said, "Yes. After everything you put him through, you should be glad that he even wants to marry me!"

Cle did not say a word.

"She's fifteen and not old enough to get married! She can't even boil water!" my mother retorted.

Why did she say those things? My dislike for her grew at that moment. Cle was trying to do the respectful and honorable thing, but her unkind and discouraging response was hurtful to us both.

She made no mention of my pregnancy. She said, "If you are going to say that you will support the baby after it's born, then I will say that is the right thing to do."

"I am willing to take care of the baby," Cleveland said.

"How will you support the baby? Do you have a job?"

There was stillness in the room and a moment of silence until he replied, "No. I am a student, but I will do everything I can and, with the help of my family, provide for the baby."

He said, "Jo-Ann can live with my parents. They will take care of her and the baby."

With discontent in her voice, she replied, "Jo-Ann will not live with anyone else but me!"

Although I was surprised, hearing those words from her made me angry. We lived together almost two years and she utters those words now. I wished I had heard them years ago Why would she say that now? My mother never gave me the impression that our living together was really what she wanted. I had not been showered with love or affection. She had not asked questions about my life prior to living with her.

My likes and dislikes were never discussed. Being that I was her only child, I wondered why we did not get along. We were strangers living together, yet she didn't want me to live with anyone else.

It seemed as if she did not want me but did not want anyone else to want me. Maybe that was the reason she had left me at Sacred Heart Orphan Asylum. All in all, her words were hurtful, and my response was anger. I did not believe she said them because of any affection she felt for me.

Cle's loss for words made me uncomfortable. I saw the disappointment in his face. He stood up in an attempt to leave. I reached for his hand and stood up as well, but he pulled his hand away, walked toward the door, turned, and said, "Miss Cave, can we talk about this again some time?"

My mother replied, "No. I don't have anything else to say about the matter."

Tears welled in my eyes when he left. I went into my bedroom, lay across the bed, and cried quietly. I did not want my mother to see or hear how much she had hurt me. While I lay on the bed, I heard the front door close. I assumed my mother had gone to Aunt Berenice's house to inform her of what had taken place.

I was disappointed with my mother's decision. Cleveland and I decided to continue seeing each other anyway. We discussed our situation. We decided that I would have to drop out of high school, he would continue his education at college, and I would move in with his parents. When I informed my mother of our plans, she was furious.

"I told you before, you're not going to live anyplace but here, and I don't want you to see that boy again!"

"All of a sudden, you're concerned about where I live!" I retorted. "You were never concerned about that before!"

"Don't talk back to me. I'm your mother," she reprimanded.

"*Now* you are my mother!" I yelled as I went into my bedroom and slammed the door so I would not hear her response. She did not follow me.

After that day, my mother and I did not have much to say to each other. She would tell me what she wanted done in the house, and I would do it. I made an effort to stay away from the house as much as possible when she was there. When I got up in the mornings, I would straighten up, clean the kitchen, and go over to Aunt Berenice's house, where I would stay all day doing chores or running errands. One day while I was at Aunt Berenice's house, I asked if I could live with her. I told her I did not want to live with my mother anymore. All I did was clean, eat, and sleep there anyway.

Aunt Berenice said, "First, I will have to talk with your mother and uncle John about this."

I thought my family's disapproval of Cle stemmed from our five-year age difference; however, there were times I wondered if there could be some kind of animosity between the two families. Whatever their reason, it didn't thwart Cle and my relationship. We sought each other out, and the more time we shared together, the closer we grew. Our union was not conceived or nourished through traditional dating or courting and marriage rituals. We embraced and enjoyed every stolen moment. When with Cle, I laughed a lot, sometimes so hard I was in tears. Other times tears were brought on by discussing family relationships. He listened to and comforted me.

One memorable sunny afternoon, we sat under the park pavilion sharing stories. Although the sun was blocked, my somber mood was not.

"I don't know why my mother doesn't like me," I said.

"Why do you say that?" Cle asked.

"Well, instead of feelings of warmth and love with my mother, it's more of a heartless emotion. We share space and talk. But we never talk about anything of substance. When our eyes meet, she looks through me with a coldness." I sighed.

Before I could say another word, Cle lifted my flip-flopped foot. He wiggled my big toe. "This little girl lived in an orphanage and had the nerve to run away."

Cle winked as he wiggled the next toe. "This little girl lived in a foster home where she wanted to stay."

Tightly squeezing another, he said, "This little girl lived with her mother and cried woe with me every day."

"Ouch! That hurts." I frowned and jerked my foot away. He rolled his eyes and grinned. It was then we looked at each other and laughed.

A few days later, while I was washing dishes at Aunt Berenice's house, she said, "Jo-Ann, I spoke with your mother and your uncle John, and we have decided you can live with us after you have your baby—but you must obey our rules. As long as you live under our roof, you cannot see or spend any time with Cle. Do you understand that?"

"Yes," I replied.

"You can share Wimpy's bedroom with her until she leaves for college."

In August 1962, at the age of sixteen, I gave birth to a beautiful son, whom I named Ramon. His caramel skin, jet-black hair, and thick eyebrows resembled those of his father. I held him in my arms, rubbed his soft, tiny arms, and touched each finger of his hands—and did the same with his legs and toes. I couldn't take my eyes away from him.

At that moment I said to myself, "This is my son, and no matter what happens in my life, I will never leave him."

As soon as I gave birth to my son, I was ready to move in with Aunt Berenice and Uncle John. No sooner had I moved in with them than my mother moved to a one-bedroom apartment several blocks away. She must have made those arrangements prior to the birth of my son. My baby did not seem to faze her one way or the other. Her main concern seemed to be with her move. She agreed to give Aunt Berenice a certain amount of money each month for letting me live there. I was really grateful for that. It seemed so easy for her to pack her things and leave, which made me think that she didn't care about me and never did. My perception of the situation verified that she didn't want me—what I had thought all along was reinforced.

I always knew that once my baby was born, I would take him to Cleveland's home. I wanted him and his parents to see the baby. His parents were more receptive to me than my family was to him. It was not long before I took my baby to see them, and then I began taking him there on a regular basis. Once Aunt Berenice found out what I had been doing, she forbade me to go back there. I loved Aunt Berenice but did not agree with her decision, so I continued to defy her. Every time I took my baby for a walk in his stroller, I would end up at Cleveland's home. His parents would fawn over my baby and mention every part of his body that resembled that of their son. My relatives disapproved of Cleveland, and that is why Cleveland and my union wasn't conceived or nourished with traditional dating and marriage rituals. The five-year age difference was brought up on more than one occasion. I never knew if or what other reason there might have been; however, their disapproval didn't prevent our connection. Every stolen moment we shared was precious, and when we weren't together, he was always on my mind. At times I would volunteer to go to the store in order to get a glimpse of him at the park. The more my relatives tried to keep us apart, the stronger our commitment to each other grew. We totally enjoyed each other. There was his hand wiping away my tears when I spoke about my early childhood. I would look up, our eyes would meet, and all my unhappy thoughts and feelings would be released. Those particular moments with Cle were pure happiness and very memorable.

A friend of my aunt and uncle who was a neighbor of Mr. and Mrs. Barrett told Aunt Berenice about my visits. Upon my return from one of our walks, Aunt Berenice confronted me with, "Jo-Ann, I told you that while you are living under my roof, you have to obey my rules. If you don't, you cannot live here anymore. One of Cle's neighbors told me that you have been taking the baby over there."

"Aunt Berenice, I think Cle and his parents should be able to see his baby."

"You are not living with Cle and his parents. You live with me."

At that moment I knew I would disobey her again. As soon as I got the opportunity, I told Cle what my aunt had said, and he suggested I move in with his parents. I was unsure how his parents would react to his suggestion but was surprised by their acceptance of the idea. The next time I took my baby to Cleveland's home, I stayed.

His parents welcomed my son and me into their home and accepted us as members of their family. Living with them was a very educational experience for me. I learned about planting vegetables and raising chickens, roosters, and rabbits—which they kept in pens in their backyard. People would come to their home to purchase all those things. His mother cooked foods I had never eaten before or even knew. She cooked greens, pig's feet, chitterlings, and many other foods strange to me. Also CH even introduced me to coffee. Everyone called Mr. Barrett, "CH" and Mrs. Barrett, "Ms. Grace" or "Gracie."

When they opened their home to me and my son, they introduced me to a whole new way of life. They were farmers who planted acres of various peppers and squash. They were in the fields before the sun rose and in the fields when the sun set. They even owned several lots not far from their house where they planted collard greens, bell peppers, and squash, which they sold to people in the neighborhood. Moonshine and whiskey were big sellers for them too. I had never heard of moonshine before living with them. Cleveland's father would keep the moonshine buried in the backyard. I later learned the reason for that was because moonshine was illegal to buy or sell, and it was illegal to sell whiskey out of your home.

My relationship with his parents was great. They treated my son and me with love and respect. They were kind people who worked hard day and night, but they still took the time to make us feel at home. While they were at work, I would clean the house, but I never cooked. I really did not know how to cook—especially the foods they ate. However, I would make a pot of coffee early in the morning before they left for the fields and another when they returned home. No matter how hot the temperature, CH would drink his coffee. He always had a pot of coffee on the stove while he was home. When he finished drinking one pot of coffee, he would immediately make another.

One day while CH was drinking his coffee, he asked, "Do you drink coffee?"

"No. My mother drinks it all the time, but I never had any," I replied.

He poured some into his saucer and handed it to me. I looked at him with a confused look but took it. "Sip this, and see how you like it," he said.

I sipped. It tasted bittersweet. It had a lot of milk and sugar in it. "It tastes OK," I said and drank all that was in the saucer.

After that day whenever he had a cup of coffee, he would pour some into his saucer for me. It was not long afterward that whenever he poured a cup, I would pour a cup for myself. CH drank coffee like it was water. The only time I saw him with water was before they went to the fields. He would prepare a gallon jug of water to take with them. They also took crackers and lunchmeat to eat while they were out in the fields.

I enjoyed the evenings we sat on the porch and drank coffee while Ms. Grace was in the kitchen cooking. CH would talk about his family and having lived in Georgia. A customer who wanted to make a purchase would interrupt his story. Whatever Ms. Grace was doing, she would stop once she heard the voice of a customer. She would engage them in long conversation, sometimes forgetting she had food on the stove.

Ms. Grace loved to talk and hear all the latest gossip. No matter what the age of her adult female customer, she always started her sentence with "Child, did you know…" or "Child, did you hear about…" But if her customer was male, she would start the sentence with "Hey, Buster," or whatever his or her name. Sometimes when families sent their children to purchase vegetables, she would ask them questions about what their mother or father was doing. She always had a nice message for the children to take back to their parents.

CH would talk with the customer whenever he could get a word in. He was more laid-back than Ms. Grace. After a hard day's work in the fields, he relaxed with his cup of coffee and Prince Albert tobacco, waiting for whatever Ms. Grace cooked. One thing that impressed me about CH was that he never drank any of the alcohol he sold—even though they had plenty of it. Sometimes a customer would come to the house to buy a pint, half pint, or a shot of whiskey and would sit on the front porch talking while he or she enjoyed the drink.

Many times the customers would come to purchase one shot, but before they left the house, they might have bought three or four. I thought they should have purchased a bottle in the first place. There were other times when customers came to purchase vegetables and decided to have a drink or two before they left. I do not know how CH and Ms. Grace were able to get up so early in the morning, because people would come to their house at all hours of the night— sometimes getting them up from bed. Their work was never done.

Ms. Grace and other people who lived in that town did something I thought strange. They routinely attended funerals, whether or not they knew the person who was deceased. Whenever Ms. Grace was not working in the fields and there was a funeral, she would put on her black dress and big, black hat and attend the funeral. Those were the only times I saw Ms. Grace dressed up. I do not know if they attended funerals out of respect or for other reasons. Many times when Ms. Grace returned home from a funeral, she would talk about how many people were in attendance, how the family reacted, how the deceased was dressed, what the preacher said, and more. I had never attended a funeral, so I would not have known what to expect. I often wondered why they attended all those funerals, but for some unknown reason, I couldn't bring myself to ask. Was routinely attending funerals a southern ritual, or did it occur everywhere?

# PART III

# ADULTHOOD

## CHAPTER TWENTY-THREE

# LOSS OF A LOVED ONE

Four beautiful children, two boys and two girls, were conceived and born during our common-law marriage. Our first daughter, Denise, was born in 1963. Her pink complexion was more prominent with that curly black hair framing her face. Small, slanted eyes and high cheekbones added to the perfection of her doll-like face.

Several months after her birth, I dressed her up in a pretty yellow dress bordered with white frills and a yellow and white bonnet. I wanted to take a picture of Denise and her father. We went outside, and Cle held her up in his arms. She leaned against his chest, and the bright yellow against the maroon and gray backdrop of his sweater was picturesque. Cle kissed her forehead and said, "Her skin is so pink; from now on, her nickname is Pinkie." That nickname remains to this day.

Our second son was born in 1965, and I suggested we name him Cleveland after his father. It was Cle's decision not to name his son Junior. "If there is going to be a junior in any family, it should always be the first son, not the second," Cle said. So our son was named Cleveland without the junior suffix.

I gave birth to our fourth child and second daughter in 1967. She was a beautiful baby with a full-head of curly, jet black hair. When I looked at her adorable face I saw Cle and myself. We pondered over names for our newborn before deciding we would name her Thursday Ann. She was born on a Thursday. We enjoyed our precious daughter for only two months before she passed away one night during her sleep. That was the first, but unfortunately not the last, time I had experienced the death of a loved one.

Our common-law marriage was abruptly terminated by Cleveland's sudden death. My father-in-law woke me on the night of July 10, 1968, to inform me that my husband had died in a car accident that day. My hysteria woke my three children. All I could do was to send them back to bed. They obeyed reluctantly. Once I had calmed down, I asked numerous questions but was not satisfied with any of the answers. I told my father-in-law that I did not believe it and would not until I saw for myself; it had to be a mistake. Even after being notified by the jurisdictional police that I would have to identify the remains, I refused to believe that the remains of which they spoke were my husband. I did not tell my children about their father's death because I was in a state of denial.

I welcomed the six-hour drive with my in-laws to Bunnell, Florida. When we arrived at the police station, we were taken to identify the vehicle. At that moment my most dreadful thoughts became realities. The sight of the vehicle jarred my insides. I left the morgue identity process to my in-laws.

Our return trip was more painful because I had the proof that I sought. I was angry. I had no idea what to do or in which direction to turn—a young twenty-two-year-old mother of three children left to raise them alone. All family decisions had been made by us both. He had always been there for us. Now he was suddenly snatched away. At twenty-seven, he was in the prime of his life. He was young, healthy, strong, and energetic with a bright future. His death was so unfair. He loved his family. Why was he taken away from us? When he died, I felt as if part of me died with him. He left me with something more meaningful than money could ever buy—cherished memories and a part of him in my children.

I finally resigned myself to the fact that I had three children dependent on me and my anger would only hinder our lives. It was imperative that I find some direction in my life. Prayer was what got me through that difficult time. I did not say the prayers that I had learned at Sacred Heart; I just openly talked to God and asked for His help. I begged Him to let me live long enough to raise my children to adulthood. I promised that I would be the best mother that I could and that I would never abandon them. I believe God looked upon my faults and saw to my needs. He continually showered me with blessings that were not a result of my good works or deeds; rather, they were portions of His mercy and kindness. Cleveland's death was such an overwhelming tragedy for me to cope with. I learned that there were no set rules or procedures to help me conquer the grief and pain. Only God's grace and glory would—and did—help me survive.

Several months after Cleveland's death, I had the pleasure of meeting his half brother and half sister. His brother's name was Charles, and his sister's name was Magnolia. Charles resembled CH, so I thought Magnolia must have resembled her mother. At that time they were visiting CH, their father. CH had previously mentioned his prior marriage and children, but their visit was a surprise to everyone. I liked them both immediately. They were cordial, friendly, and very interesting people. By the time they had been there a few days, we were acting as if we were long lost relatives who had rediscovered each other. I was just as interested in their lives as they were in mine.

They asked me about my future plans, and Magnolia asked if I intended to remain in Florida. I really did not like living in Florida, but I was unsure of my future plans. She suggested I visit Illinois to see if I would like living there. She invited me to visit her for a couple weeks. I accepted her invitation. When they returned to Rockford, Illinois, I made arrangements to visit them. Once in Rockford, I decided it was a great place to raise a family. I met Chuck's wife and three children. Magnolia had one daughter, who was married and had a son. I really enjoyed my two-week stay. Magnolia's daughter, Beatrice, and her husband, Thomas, took me to the Milwaukee Zoo and other interesting places. Thomas, a member of a motorcycle club, took me on my first motorcycle ride.

The thing that most impressed me in Rockford, Illinois, was that black and white people lived in the same neighborhoods and were not separated by railroad tracks. The last place I had lived without that kind of separation was Poughkeepsie, New York. While in Rockford, I looked for employment, took various employment tests, was hired by the state of Illinois, and given a start date. The fact that I found employment so quickly was amazing and exciting. It felt as if that whole process had been a dream. My next task was to find a place for my family to live. I thought it would be harder to find a home than it was to find a job, but with Magnolia's help, that task was much easier.

My sister-in-law thought that a small empty house across the street from her would be a good place for my family to live. She contacted the landlord and arranged for us to see it. It was a two-bedroom house with a bathroom, kitchen, and living room. After I looked at the inside of the house, I wanted to rent it. I knew I could afford the rent and asked if he would accept a deposit that day and payment of the balance upon my return. He agreed to this arrangement. The best part about the entire prospect was the location of the house and its affordability. My family and I would feel safe moving to a new city and living near relatives. That entire move would not have been possible without Magnolia's assistance. I never would have known that house was available, because it had no rental sign. Magnolia knew it was empty because of where she lived.

So Thomas and Beatrice's efforts made it possible for me to find employment, and, to top all of that off, Magnolia helped me find a place for my family to live. It was great having a supportive family!

My entire two-week vacation was not only enjoyable but also very eventful. Thomas and Beatrice drove me around town sight-seeing and introduced me to some wonderful people. Prior to that time, I had never taken a vacation, but that vacation could not have been better. When the time came for me to leave, I was sad, but at the same time, I could not wait to get back to Florida to pack and move my family to Illinois.

Rockford, Illinois, was like a whole new world compared to Dania, Florida. I never liked the separation of people because of their color in the south. Also I did not find very much to do in Dania other than go to the beach, and I definitely was not a beach person. The only time I went to the beach other than with Cle was once with Uncle John and Aunt Berenice. Being out in the hot sun on the hot sand was not much fun to me. I never could understand why people enjoyed playing and lying on the hot beach.

Immediately upon my return to Florida, I informed CH and Ms. Gracie about my plans to move to Illinois. It made them very unhappy. They told me I was too young to move that far with three small children and asked if I would leave my children with them. I felt very strongly that I would never leave my children. My decision to move was made, and nothing or no one would change my mind. CH and Ms. Gracie had been wonderful to my children and me. I could not have asked for better grandparents for my children or in-laws for myself, but it was time for a change.

I submitted a resignation notice to the *Sun Tattler* newspaper, where I worked as a classified-ad typist, and prepared for our move. I rented a U-Haul truck and hired a driver who would drive our belongings to Rockford, Illinois. Also I bought our plane tickets. We flew into Chicago, where we were met at the airport by Magnolia. My children and I temporarily moved into her home, located on the quiet street with trees where we would soon live. Her house was quaint with a basement where she kept canned fruits and vegetables and had her washing machine and dryer. My children and I enjoyed living with her and her husband, Frank. She cooked delicious foods and baked the best pies I had ever eaten. We often sat under a huge weeping willow tree in her backyard, talking about our family and many other things. She introduced me to her neighbors who were very friendly and welcomed us into the neighborhood.

Magnolia taught me how to play different board games—Yahtzee being her favorite. Whenever we had free time and were not enjoying ourselves sitting under that big, beautiful weeping willow tree, we would be in the house playing Yahtzee. Magnolia even taught my children how to play that game—which they enjoyed as much as we did. Prior to moving to Rockford, we had never played board games.

When the truck arrived with our belongings, Magnolia, Beatrice, and Thomas helped us move into our home. I enjoyed living with Magnolia and Frank, but the fact that we were moving into our own place was exciting. Moving had been part of my life since childhood. I do not remember where I lived prior to my move to a home for girls. I moved in with the Johnsons from the home for girls and then another institutional home and back to the girls' home. From there, I moved in with Uncle Nick and Aunt Madeline, and from there, I went to live with my mother. I moved out from my mother to live with Aunt Berenice and Uncle John. After my first son was born, I moved in with the Barretts, and from there, I moved to our own apartment. My next move was to live with Magnolia and her husband. Finally I was ready for the biggest move of all—to move with my children into a place we could call our own.

The house was small, but the children would have a safe place to play because there were both front and back yards. The front yard was larger than the backyard, and the children could be easily seen when they were outside playing. Magnolia could also see them from her house when they played in the front yard.

We enjoyed our new home and surroundings. My children met other children who lived in the neighborhood and immediately made new friends. I continued to visit Magnolia on a daily basis to eat, sit down, and talk or play board games. We lived in that house for almost a year. It took that long for me to get acclimated to the town and my job. I realized the house was too small when we moved in, but there could not have been a better location for my family to live upon our arrival to town.

Eventually we had to admit we needed more space and it was time for my children to have separate bedrooms. With the help of Magnolia, I located a larger, affordable brick home located on Stanley Street in a nice neighborhood. The house had a kitchen, dining room, living room, one bedroom and bathroom downstairs, and three bedrooms upstairs. My children no longer had to share a bedroom. Also, there was a large backyard where they could play. All the houses on that street were large but very different from each other. The houses in our previous neighborhood were very similar. The children were enrolled in their new public school which was walking distance from our home. They did well in their new school and met new friends. Some of their friends lived on Stanley Street as well.

We had been enjoying our new home for almost a year when I received a call from Aunt Berenice informing me that my mother had a drinking problem. Caring for my mother in that condition was too problematic, given that her immediate family had to be her priority. Aunt Berenice wanted to know if I had enough room in my home to accommodate my mother. I thought about the unpleasant, short period of time I had lived with my mother. I was hesitant to accept her into my home. We had not spoken to each other for several years, and now she drank. After much deliberation, however, I agreed. After all, she was my mother.

Aunt Berenice made all the arrangements, and several weeks later, I met my mother at O'Hare Airport in Chicago.

"How was your flight?" I asked.

"That was my first time flying, and I was a little nervous," she replied.

When we were in Rockford, I pointed out sites I thought would be of interest to her. My sight-seeing remarks prevented total silence.

"We're not far from the house. Do you want or need anything from the store before we get home?" I asked.

"Yes, let's stop so I can buy some cigarettes."

We stopped at the grocery store, which was about seven blocks from home. She purchased a carton of cigarettes and several other items.

I showed her around the house. In the kitchen, I opened the full refrigerator and told her she could cook or prepare whatever she wanted. Upstairs we entered her room. This was a unique situation. I wondered if she was feeling all the emotions I had felt that day I had entered her home for the very first time. Back then I wanted nothing more than to be with her in her home, but it had felt cold and unwelcoming. Now the tide had turned, and I wanted to make her experience more pleasant than mine had been. Unfortunately, I didn't know how.

Within a couple weeks, she had obtained a job cooking at a restaurant. She worked there five days per week, which she seemed to enjoy. At home, she talked about things that happened at the job on that particular day. When not talking about her job, she sat on the front steps or back porch smoking. I never mentioned what Aunt Berenice had told me about her drinking; however, one Friday she came home with a case of beer. She placed the beer in the refrigerator before going upstairs to her room. A short time later, she came downstairs, got a beer, and took it outside onto the back porch. Most of her weekends were spent sitting on the back porch drinking beer. My mother only drank on weekends, but that never resulted in her being late to work on Monday morning or missing a day of work.

Several times when I looked out the kitchen window, I saw her talking to one of our neighbors. Although he lived around the corner from us, our backyards were separated by a fence. Sometimes she stood there talking to him with a cigarette in her hand. I had not met that neighbor until the day he knocked on my door. I was more than a little surprised when I opened the door.

"Hello," he said. "I'm Sydney and I live around the corner. You must be Jo-Ann."

Before I could respond, he said, "I am here to pick up Ruth. I'm taking her out to dinner."

Seeing him at my door was a surprise, but learning that he was taking my mother to dinner was a bit of a shock. Although he was my neighbor, we had not previously met. I looked him over quickly but thoroughly. He was an attractive, well-dressed man.

"Come in, Mr. Sydney. Please have a seat," I said.

"Thank you. Is Ruth here?" he asked.

"Yes. She's upstairs. I'll let her know you're here," I said. I ran upstairs and knocked on my mother's door. "Mr. Sydney's downstairs."

"OK, I'll be right down."

When I entered the room, he smiled pleasantly. I returned a smile and said, "My mother will be down in a minute." I decided to engage him in small talk while he waited for my mother. "You're the man who lives in the gray house around the corner, aren't you?" I asked.

"Yes. I live there with my mother and sister," he replied.

"I'm glad to meet another neighbor," I said.

"Likewise," Sydney said. "I don't remember seeing you in the neighborhood. How long have you lived here?"

"Not long."

"How long is not long?"

I smiled and replied, "Not quite a year."

"I haven't seen you in the neighborhood or even in your backyard before."

"Well, I work during the week, and I don't spend any time in the backyard."

Mr. Sydney had a cordial disposition and spoke softly, and I immediately liked him. He and my mother went out several times after that day. They seemed to enjoy each other's company. I was glad my mother met someone she could spend time with when not at her job.

Sidney and my mother continued to socialize. He came to the house to see or pick up my mother on a regular basis; however, the majority of the time it was to get her so that they could go out someplace. Their relationship developed into more than friendship. Months later my mother informed me that she and Sydney were moving into an apartment together. I was happy for them. Sydney was a good man whom I liked and respected.

## CHAPTER TWENTY-FOUR

# A FATHER FIGURE?

Five years after my husband's death, I was introduced to Willie Washington, who would become my second husband. I thought he was a very interesting person with a great sense of humor. The differences between him and my first husband were substantial. Willie's middle name was Earl, and that was what everyone called him. He liked to go to bars and clubs to drink, dance, and party. Cleveland, on the other hand, enjoyed being home and doing things with his family.

Shortly after our introduction, we began dating. I think his carefree attitude is what actually attracted me to him. His looks were OK, but his appearance wasn't even close to that of my first husband. He had a great personality, and my children liked him. After we had dated about six months, he asked me to marry him. I was twenty-seven years old at the time. I discussed the idea with my children, and they agreed to go along with whatever I wanted to do. Prior to our meeting, I had been begun to have problems raising three children. I thought the problems stemmed from their not having a father in the home. I thought that if they had a father figure, their behavior would improve. They seemed to like Earl, as did I, but I did not love him. When he asked me to marry him, however, I thought that would be the logical move to benefit my children.

Earl's family was not too enthusiastic about him marrying a woman with three children. Once his relatives realized that they could not influence our decision, they accepted the fact that we would marry. His family and I got along well together. I believe his mother and father thought that I brought some stability into Earl's life. Earl and I realized that we were total opposites, and maybe that was some of the attraction. He was outgoing and liked to party. I was more reserved and family-oriented. I overlooked our differences. I thought our differences would enhance our relationship, making it interesting and exciting, and that we could work around any problems that might arise. My expectations for that marriage were that my children would have a father figure in the home and our family would have financial security and stability.

Our union resulted in many adjustments for us all. Earl became an instant parent, and his lifestyle changed totally. He lived in Joliet, Illinois, so my children and I moved once again. Prior to our move, I was able to transfer my employment, because the state agency, Illinois Department of Public Aid, for which I worked, had an office in Joliet. I worked there for a few years. My children adjusted to having another adult in the home and to asking his permission for various things. Sometimes, when they did not like his decision, they would come to me, hoping my decision would be different. Prior to the marriage, I was very independent. None of my decisions concerning myself and my children were questioned by anyone.

With so many changes at one time, conflict surrounded some adjustments. The fact that Earl and I had very little in common did not help the situation at all. He enjoyed going to nightclubs, and I joined him on many occasions. But I preferred going to the movies or to the park or whatever we could enjoy as a family. He liked baseball, and my favorite sport was football. He had a good-paying job, but he was not interested in advancing his career or furthering his education. I also had a good job, but I had a hunger for more. This spurred me to seek better opportunities. Once I worked at Joliet Junior College, and then I got a job working at the Crime Lab in Joliet—another state agency. It was difficult for me to understand why Earl did not want to improve his professional life.

After I worked at the Crime Lab for about a year, my sisters-in-law suggested I try to get hired where they worked—for the federal government at the Atomic Energy Commission, located at Argonne National Laboratory. They invited me to carpool with them if I was hired. I applied and was hired for a secretarial position. We did indeed carpool. Each of us drove to work for one week at a time. I enjoyed working at Argonne National Laboratory and had a great boss, Gary Pitchford, who was a director. That job was the most interesting that I had ever worked, and I learned so much. Eventually I decided to return to school for personal and professional growth.

Thoughts of what I wanted to accomplish in my working career were always on my mind. I knew I did not want to be a secretary forever. The most interesting career that came to mind at that time was court stenography. The nearest schools that taught court stenography were located in Chicago, Illinois. I did not want to drive to Chicago on a daily basis, so I looked into modes of transportation and discovered there were daily train and bus routes into Chicago. After a little research, I selected the school I wanted to attend and applied for admission. All students were informed they could not work while taking the court-stenographer course. I talked about it with Earl, and we agreed that I would quit my job to attend school full-time.

The daily one and one-half hour train commute to Chicago allowed me time to read and study. Another student in my class commuted to Chicago as well, and often we sat together. The course was very demanding and required the purchase of a stenograph machine. Many nights I took the machine to bed with me to practice and fell asleep with it. The course included classes in such things as legal and medical terminology. I completed the course and took the required certification exam. I passed one part of the exam but failed another. I had an opportunity to retake the exam, but I never did. At the time I felt that if I had failed a part of the exam while I was still attending school and using the stenograph machine every day, it would be much harder for me to pass the exam when school had been completed and I was not using or practicing using my machine every day.

It was time for me to find a job so I could contribute to our household. I planned to look for a job that did not require secretarial work. I had taken medical terminology as one of my courses and decided to seek employment as a medical transcriber. I applied at the two hospitals in Joliet and worked at St. Joseph Hospital for a short time. I even worked part-time transcribing medical reports at a doctor's private office. While attending school in Chicago, I enjoyed the commute, so I decided to seek employment in the big city. I applied for a position at a large medical center, passed their medical-terminology test, and was hired. My pay was more at that one job than it had been working two jobs in Joliet.

Commuting was exciting, and I saw and met some very interesting people. Some were friendly, and some were not. It got to the point where I began to sit in the same train car in the same location almost daily. I sat on a car that would be closer to the terminal upon my arrival in Chicago. I commuted by train for several years. After the train arrived in downtown Chicago, I rode a bus to the medical center. Eventually I learned that the bus commute would be more convenient and less expensive. I rode the bus to Chicago, and there was an el train stop located a block from where I got off the bus. In addition there was a family restaurant in the area where some of us would stop to buy a cup of coffee or breakfast before we continued on our way to work. None of the other people with whom I commuted from Joliet worked at the medical center. They worked at various locations in Chicago. I rode the el train, that made a stop right at the medical center. It could not have been better for me, and I continued that manner of commuting for some time.

## CHAPTER TWENTY-FIVE

# A HOUSE IS NOT A HOME

Earl and I made the important decision to purchase a home. Naively I thought that purchasing a home would improve our family relationship. This happened briefly, but our relationship lacked love and trust—the basics. I did not trust him because of his previous lifestyle and because of some dynamics in our relationship. Also I couldn't help but compare him to Cleveland. My children explicitly did the same. My youngest son once said to Earl, "I'm going to be just like my father. I'm not going to drink, and I'm not going to smoke." He was only three years old when his father died. My children's father made an everlasting impression on them—for which I was thankful.

My second marriage taught me the real value of my first one. Shared friendship, love, trust, and common interests should be the basis for a life partnership. Another thing I learned was the importance of choosing a mate for myself—not for the benefit or satisfaction of others. If I had realized how my second marriage would unfold, I never would have married for the reasons that I did. First of all, I was not fair to Earl, because I did not love him. Secondly, I was unfair to my children for trying to replace their father—especially with someone who was so totally different. Last, I was unfair to myself for getting into a relationship that did not have the potential to last and one that put me in a vulnerable situation.

About once a month I would drive to Rockford so that my children could see their grandmother. I guess that was my way of inadvertently checking on her. She continued to work, but did not discontinue drinking. Sydney seemed to be a mild-mannered man. He never raised his voice nor showed displeasure when my mother drank. If he drank, it was never in my presence. When we visited my mother, we would all go out to eat. Sometimes she or Sydney paid for our meal, and other times I did. My children called Sydney "Mr. Sydney." Earl didn't accompany us on our trips to Rockford. We usually went on a Saturday, when he was either working overtime or had other plans.

A few years after our move to Joliet, Sydney passed away. My mother continued to live and work in Rockford. And I continued my visits to see her, but they were less frequent.

To my surprise, one day I received a telephone call from one of my mother's friends informing me that my mother had been drinking a lot—and that I needed to go see about her. Her friend suggested that when I got to town to call her because, more than likely, my mother would be at her home. I arrived in Rockford to find my mother in a drunken stupor. Unable to engage her in lucid conversation, my attention was suddenly shifted to the voice coming from the kitchen, which said, "Recently your mother has been drinking more than usual."

"What's considered usual?" I asked.

"She's gotten to the point where she is drinking on a daily basis."

"Has she missed any time at work because of it?"

"I don't know, but if she keeps on like this, she won't have a job to go to. I've tried talking to her about it, but I'm not getting through to her. Sometimes when she comes here, I don't answer the door."

"Who buys the beer when she's over here?"

"Sometimes she brings it with her, or she'll give someone money to go to the store to buy it."

Sounding a little agitated, I retorted, "Then don't accept her money, and don't buy beer for her! I'm going to take her home, but please call me if you have any more problems."

I drove my mother to her apartment, where I remained until she fell asleep.

It wasn't long after that trip that my mother's friend called me again. She informed me that I needed to move my mother to Joliet with me. Her friend was worried about her and did not want to be responsible for her. After talking with her, I called my mother to inform her I would be there in a couple of weeks to move her to Joliet. The move was easy, because she didn't have any furniture to speak of. Earl followed me to Rockford in his car. Between the both of us, we were able to transport all of her belongings.

After she was settled into our home, she found a job at a dry cleaner not far from where we lived. It was in walking distance. After living with us about five months, my mother decided to move into the apartment of a women friend she had met. She agreed to pay half of the expenses. My mother did most of the cooking, and Mary did the baking of desserts. She baked an angel food cake for me one year for my birthday because my mother told her I liked that cake. Her angel food cake was the best I had ever tasted. I asked for the recipe, but even with her recipe, my cakes didn't taste as good. Mary seemed to be a few years older than my mother. She was a Caucasian woman who was friendly and very pleasant. They got along very well.

Mary and my mother lived together for approximately three years before Mary became ill. Her grandson, who lived in Las Vegas, decided he would move her back home with him. Once my mother learned that Mary would be moving, she made arrangements to move into a senior housing facility. Mary told my mother she could take whatever furniture she wanted except the stove and refrigerator, because they did not belong to her. Earl and I helped her move her belongings to her new apartment. The building management informed her she could move her own refrigerator and stove in the apartment if she wanted. Earl and I gave her our refrigerator and stove, because we decided to buy new ones.

## CHAPTER TWENTY-SIX

# CAUGHT IN THE ACT

Earl's lifestyle was the reason our marriage did not last; he liked to drink and party too much. On payday, he would cash his check and meet his friends at a bar. By the time he came home, he did not have a penny. One Friday payday, Earl did not come home. I decided to go to one of the bars he frequented to get some money from him. I saw his car outside the bar but didn't see him inside. The bartender told me he had not seen him and didn't know where he was.

I walked to an apartment building next door to the bar. There was a young boy about seven years old in front of the building. I pointed to the green car and asked, "Do you know the man who drives that car?"

He pointed to the door behind him. Since the door was open, I walked in. To my surprise, I saw a pair of men's shoes on the floor, pants, and shirt on the sofa, but I didn't see anyone. I asked the boy, who had followed me in, where Earl was. He pointed to a closed door. Apprehensive and nervous, I momentarily stood outside the door to gather myself. Then I opened it.

There was my husband, Earl, in the bed with a woman. Shocked, I stood motionless before anyone noticed me. She saw me first and pushed him away, pulling the sheet over herself. Only then did Earl see me.

"What the fuck are you doing in my house?" she yelled.

My response was to grab the sheet she held around her body exposing her as she jumped out of the bed. I pulled her hair, but my grip loosened when Earl got between us to pull us apart. My punches didn't connect, either, because of his interference. His penis was swinging back and forth making an excellent target. I tried to kick him in that area but was unable to connect there, either. I was angry with Earl for preventing me from beating the mess out of that woman and angry with myself for not being able to kick him where I wanted. Angrily I rushed out of her apartment shouting to Earl, "Don't bother to come back home!"

Earl did not return home for a couple days. When he did, he apologized—telling me it would not happen again. I was so angry with him that I took off my wedding ring and threw it out the window.

"This marriage is over," I said.

He went on to beg and plead with me to give him another chance. For financial reasons, I finally did give him that chance. After we argued and talked, he went outside to look for the ring, but it was never found.

In addition to Earl's wasteful spending, he eventually lost his job for missing work. I continued trying to salvage our marriage until

I learned he was using drugs. One day I came home from work to find what looked like flour on the dining-room table. I smelled it and then stuck my index finger in it and tasted it like they did on television. I knew that substance was not flour.

When Earl returned home that evening, I asked, "How long have you been using drugs?"

"I don't use drugs," he replied.

"Well, you forgot to clean your drugs off the table. Earl, I've put up with your bullshit long enough. It's time for you to leave. Take your clothes with you, or I'll throw them out!"

"Come on, Jo-Ann. I'm sorry. It won't happen again."

"I know it won't happen again in this house. Get out!"

While he stood in amazement, I called his mother and told her why I was putting her son out of our home. After that phone call, he left with some of his clothes, leaving other belongings. That was the climax of our marriage drama—with no resolution in sight.

I continued my commute to Chicago for work. Eventually I decided it would be more convenient to move there. Roger, a very good friend and coworker, lived in Chicago. He made arrangements for me to meet the owner of an apartment building to look at some apartments, and I was able to rent one on the spot.

I had been employed at the medical center for about eight years when I decided to return to school to further my education. I applied to an accelerated thirteen-month program at National Louis University. The school accepted my credits from the other colleges, which qualified me for that particular program. I graduated with honors and a bachelor of arts degree in business management. Only three students from our class graduated. The course was very stringent, but ultimately it had all been worth the struggle and hard work.

The first position I acquired after receiving my degree was as an administrative assistant, which I equate with being a glorified secretary. In all, eventually I was a clerical supervisor, medical-transcription supervisor, administrator, and center administrator, which were all very important learning experiences. All of those jobs were promotions at the same medical center.

## CHAPTER TWENTY-SEVEN

# REACHING OUT

After two marriages, three children, seventeen grandchildren, and several great-grandchildren, when I was in my sixties, I looked back on all the years wasted between my mother and me. I wish our relationship had been different. Although we shared housing at various times, there was never shared love. I couldn't convince myself to address her as "Mother" or "Mom." When in the same house but different rooms, I would raise my voice if I wanted her attention. When my-raised-voice approach didn't work, I'd wait for her to come into the same room. Why had I been so stubborn by refusing to address her appropriately when I spoke with her? How could I have let that go on so long? Whenever I spoke *about* her, she was my mother but not when speaking *to* her. I respected her and did whatever I could for her but not the thing she probably wanted most. I could not—or would not—call her "Mother" because I did not feel that kind of bond.

Expression of affection had always been missing from our relationship. I felt that lack deeply. My stubbornness prevented me from saying what might have been the most important word she could have heard from me—"Mother." The most important words I longed to hear from her were, "I love you." I don't believe we knew how to love or to verbally express our feelings. Perhaps my not calling her mother could have been some sort retaliation for all the years without having a mother in my life. Maybe she had been doing the same. I always wondered if she yearned to hear me say the word that I assumed would have meant the most to her, but my foolish pride prevented me from doing that.

However, during my forties, I finally reached the conclusion that neither of those things would ever occur. So in June 1990, I decided to write my mother a letter with some things I could not bring myself to ask or say to her in person.

Dear Mother,

There have been many times when I wanted to ask you certain questions and express my feelings and thoughts to you but did not know how or where to begin; however, I have now decided that the easiest way for me to do this is in writing. Five-year-old children love their parents, but I believe my separation from you at such an early age resulted in the fading of my affections. During my adolescent years, my yearning to have you in my life was overwhelming. The days turned into weeks and the weeks into months and then the months into years. Today I sometimes ask myself if you love me or ever have loved me. You may ask yourself why I think this way, and I'll try to explain it as best I can.

Why? I think that you do not love me because you have never told me that you love me, nor have you ever shown me any kind of affection. I don't know what it is like to be hugged, kissed or even comforted by a mother.

Why did you take me to Sacred Heart Orphan Asylum? That is my most burning question. Why did you leave me there for so many years? Every day I spent at Sacred Heart, I asked myself why I was there. I could never think of an answer that made sense to me.

Why didn't you visit me? I thought maybe your reason for not visiting me was because you could not drive and did not own a car; but there is always a way if you want to do it.

Why didn't you write to me? I would have loved to receive letters from you. I probably would not have focused so much on wanting visits from you if I had received letters. I wanted to know you were at least thinking about me.

Did you know I was sent to live in a foster home? If you did know, did you care?

Do you know why I was sent to live at a foster home? I sometimes thought I was sent to live with the Johnson family because the nuns at the home thought you were not returning to get me—or that you no longer wanted me. Why, when it was time for me to permanently leave the home, was I picked up by strangers?

Another thing that has been on my mind for many years is that you have never mentioned my father. I would like to know some things about him. Who is he? What's his name?

Where is he? Why wasn't he in my life? I would like to know everything and anything you can tell me about him. Would I ever want to meet him? I do not know, but learning some things about him would mean a lot to me.

This next question is something I have often thought about. Do I have any sisters or brothers? If so, what are their names, and where are they?

My reason for waiting so long to ask you those questions is because I kept thinking that you would eventually talk to me about those issues without me having to ask. I thought you would tell me about all these things on the day I arrived in Florida to live with you. I have come to the conclusion that it is my responsibility to ask the questions I so desperately want answered—and it's better now than never. I am writing this letter—not to hurt you—but to possibly open a line of communication between us. Your answers, regardless of what they may be or how they may make me feel, are very important to me—and necessary at this time in my life. Also it's time for the healing process to begin.

Now that I have conjured up enough nerve to ask you those questions, I sincerely hope you will answer them for me. It doesn't matter whether you reply in writing, over the phone, or in person the next time we see each other. Your response means more to me than you will ever know. Hopefully our talking about these issues will improve our understanding of each other as well as our relationship.

Love,

Jo-Ann

When I finished that letter, I felt as if weight had been lifted from my shoulders. I read it several times before sealing the envelope. After I mailed the letter, two weeks passed with no response from my mother. Over and over again, I asked myself if she had received my letter. It had not been returned to sender. I wondered if I should call her or if I should wait for her to contact me. It took over forty years for me to write that letter and ask those questions, and at that moment, I did not want to wait another day, hour, or minute.

That day when I had made up my mind to call her, my hand nervously shook as I dialed her phone number. When she answered the phone, I asked, "Did you receive the letter I sent you?"

"Yes, I got it," she replied.

I was hoping for a little excitement or anxiety in her voice, but there was none. Her lack of emotion regarding the letter was upsetting. Neither of us said a word until I broke the silence with, "What do you think about it?"

"I don't know," she said.

Because of the uneasiness I heard in her voice, I decided to change the subject.

"How have you been doing," I asked.

"I'm all right."

"How is Mary?" Mary was one of her neighbor friends who lived in the same building.

"She's OK. Her grandson is coming from Southern Illinois this weekend to visit her."

"That's nice. I'll be there to visit you next weekend, so maybe we can talk about the letter."

"OK, I'll see you next week," she replied.

At the moment I heard the click of her phone, I had an epiphany. I realized that I had asked her about the letter before I even asked how she was doing or feeling. My feelings and wants were put before her own. Was that something I had always done? Had I really not called her "Mother" because she had not given me the information I wanted or because she had not made me feel loved or wanted?

Prior to that moment, I had not thought about her feelings. It was all about me, my feelings, and the things I wanted, needed, and expected from her. I had never given thought to how she felt or what went through her mind during our ride to Sacred Heart so many years ago or even what her feelings were when that door closed as she left without me. Did she cry? Did she want to change her mind and not leave me there? What were her thoughts and feelings? All those years I had been so immersed in my own feelings that I never took or made the time to think about hers.

## CHAPTER TWENTY-EIGHT

# WORDS OF MY FATHER

During the drive to my mother's home, I wondered how I would start the conversation between us. When I reached her home, I remained in the car for several minutes trying to decide how to say what I needed to say without hurting her feelings. Unable to decide on the appropriate wording, I made the sign of the cross before exiting the car. She buzzed me into the building, but when I reached her door I paused and took a deep breath before I knocked.

When she opened the door, we looked into each other's eyes. We did not lose eye contact until I wrapped my arms around her. Tears welled in my eyes when I felt her arms around me. Neither of us said a word. My thoughts were of all our wasted years without demonstrative affection—without touch or hugs. I do not know how long we stood embracing each other, but that was a moment I had longed for all my life. I did not want it to end.

After our embrace, I tried to make eye contact, but she turned toward the kitchen. "Do you want a cup of coffee?" she asked in a tone much softer than normal.

"Sure," I replied on my way to the bathroom.

I flushed the toilet and turned on the faucet in an attempt to muffle my sobs. Why had it taken so many years for us to embrace each other? The cold water on my face was not only refreshing but calming. I returned to the living room, where my mother was sitting in the pink flowered, overstuffed chair drinking coffee and smoking a cigarette. She had already placed my cup of coffee on the table in front of the sofa. I raised my head so the warm liquid stimulated the roof of my mouth as it continued to flow down my throat.

With both hands wrapped around my coffee cup, I looked at my mother for a few minutes and asked, "Why did you take me to Sacred Heart Orphan Asylum?"

I did not learn the full name of the institution until many years later. During the time I resided there, it was known as Sacred Heart Home.

"I had to work and didn't have anyone to take care of you while I worked," she replied.

"You didn't know anyone who could take care of me—not even family—for nine years?"

She looked down, "No. I worked hard to pay for you to attend Sacred Heart. I paid twenty dollars a month, which was a lot of money back then."

"There were many days I wished you had come to visit me," I said with my voice cracking. "Why? Why didn't you visit me?"

Several minutes passed without a response.

"Did you ever think about writing to me?"

She did not respond.

"Before a few minutes ago, we had never even hugged each other. We have never shown affection toward each other."

"I wasn't hugged or kissed when I was growing up, either. I was the black sheep of my family," she said.

"But what does that have to do with us?" I asked.

Realizing I was not going to get an answer, I changed the subject. "Well, what about my father? You never mentioned him or told me anything about him."

"Your father was twenty-eight years older than me when we married. He had been previously married and had five daughters with his first wife. His name is Joe. He worked in Harlem as a gas-station attendant located on One Hundred Twenty-Fifth Street under the train line. We lived at One Hundred Thirty-Fourth Street between Lenox and Fifth Avenue."

She stared directly into my eyes and said, "Your father left me when you were six weeks old. The last words he said before he left me were, 'If the baby gets cold, open the window, and if she gets hungry, feed her water.' I never saw him again after that."

She spouted those words with such venom, and the cold stare of her eyes added to the internal pain I felt. How could such words garner so much passion in her voice without visibly betraying emotion. Maybe the conviction I heard in her voice was relief for finally letting it out after having held it in for all those years. I watched her eyes shift slightly as she exhaled and stubbed out her half-smoked cigarette.

If she was looking for a reaction from me, there was none. My body was physically unable to respond. My eyes were moist and my breathing quicker, but I felt numb. My heart was pierced when I heard those awful words that a father was to have said about his child.

I sat silently for a while, not knowing what to say. For an instant, I wondered if my father really had said those words. Also, I wondered why my mother told me. Was it because she was mad with him for leaving her? Or was she angry with me and wanted to hurt me? I had no way of verifying what she had told me, but the coldness in her stare hurt almost as much as the words that came from her mouth.

My stomach was twisting in knots. Surprise and anger were all I could feel after hearing what she said. Suddenly I slumped back against the sofa, closed my eyes, and inhaled deeply. I thought, *Wow! Did he really say if I get hungry, to feed me water and, if I get cold, to open the window? Evidently he didn't care what happened to me. He did not want me and did not care what happened to me.*

I slowly exhaled, not knowing what to say after having just gotten the shock of my life. My eyes remained closed with a myriad of thoughts going through my mind until they were disrupted with, "Do you want more coffee?"

The way my stomach was churning, I did not know if I would be able to drink another cup of coffee, but I handed her the cup anyway. At that moment I felt as empty as that cup.

I was deeply saddened to hear that my father had spoken those words. Before I had driven to my mother's home that day, I had thought I was prepared to hear anything—but I was wrong. Nothing could have prepared me for what I heard. Throughout my childhood and adulthood, I believed my mother never wanted me or cared about me. In the past, I had always felt that my father did not want me, but hearing what he had said really struck a nerve. Those beliefs I held about my mother and father affected every aspect of my life—from how I acted and behaved as a child, to the relationship between my mother and me, to my relationship with my own children.

When I was twenty-two years old, without a husband and with three children to raise, I was preparing to move to the state of Illinois. My in-laws told me that I was too young to move away and raise three children alone. They asked me if I would leave my children with them in Florida, but I refused. When my children were born, I had promised myself that I would never leave them or allow them to be raised by anyone but me. I knew all too well what it was like not to be raised by a parent. Although my children were loved by their grandparents and would have been given good care, I would never leave them.

No child should hear that a parent doesn't care whether he or she lived or died. I almost wished she had not told me—I couldn't erase the words. Years earlier, if my mother had told me what my father had said, I don't know how I might have reacted. Perhaps in addition to being shocked, I would have cried, shouted, screamed, and maybe thrown things, but I doubt I could have been any angrier than I was at that moment. No matter how awful I felt when I heard of my father's indifference, I would not allow myself to react demonstrably. Why should I allow someone who did not care whether I lived or died control my emotions? I did not want to show emotion in front of my mother, either, because I did not want her to see me cry or know how I truly felt.

Suddenly I wondered how she must have felt hearing those words. She had a child with a man who let her know he did not care about her child's well-being. Was that her reason for taking me to Sacred Heart? Did she blame me for his leaving? Maybe she thought he would return if she did not have me in her life. Wow! As those thoughts passed through my mind, I sipped my coffee. Coffee was not what I needed at that time, I thought. I swallowed my last sip and got up. There was no use thinking about those things anymore.

"Do you need anything from the store or want me to run any errands for you before I leave?" I asked.

"No, I don't need anything," my mother responded.

Although there were many questions left to ask—and the timing probably right—I could not go on. I was done.

My driving speed increased with each thought racing through my mind. But when I looked at the speedometer and saw how fast I was driving, I slammed on my brakes, and all thoughts halted. I checked my rearview mirror and did not see any cars close behind me.

"Slow down, and focus on getting home in one piece," is what I told myself. The drive home that afternoon seemed to take much longer than usual, even though I drove faster. When I got home, I turned off the ignition and wrapped my arms around the steering wheel with my head resting against it. I could not hold back the tears any longer.

I do not remember walking up the three flights of stairs to my apartment that afternoon. Also I do not remember eating anything. The rest of that afternoon and evening was a blank. But I do recall that most of that night was spent alternating between the bed and sofa. I hugged that pillow so tightly—as though trying to squeeze life from it. Was I subconsciously substituting the pillow for my father? His haunting words were reverberating in my head, causing it to ache. The more I thought about what he had said, the tighter I squeezed the pillow. When I awakened the next morning, I was surprised to find myself wrapped around the intact pillow. The way I had treated it, the pillow's insides should have been all over my bed.

I lay in bed, lost in thoughts of the past. I thought about the times at Sacred Heart we had scavenger hunts and ran all over the place looking for a hidden object. We even searched through the apple orchards. During those times, our young minds never imagined that the apple orchards were too far away for the nuns to hide an object, but we had fun looking for it. The times we walked and played for approximately four or five miles "up the mountain" were fun. When we reached the top, we gathered at a shrine and prayed. After that we were given a snack—usually a piece of fruit—and then made our way back down the mountain. It always took us longer to go up than to come down, but we enjoyed ourselves.

There was a room outside of our playroom that contained what seemed like hundreds of skates. We picked our own. Some were buckled together, and others were not. We were always told to buckle our skates together when we were finished with them. There were just as many unbuckled as were buckled. I always tried to put my skates in a particular area of the room when I finished skating so that I could get the same pair of skates the next time. No matter how many times I did that, it never worked. Roller-skating races were exciting. Two girls at a time raced down the paved road toward the stone wall. Another exciting time for me was when we walked down the mountain to swim. I did not realize that swimming in the Hudson River was a big deal until many years after leaving that home. When I told other people about where we swam, they did not believe me. I really don't know why they didn't believe me. Did swimming in the Hudson River sound too outrageous?

Those were just some of the many good times I enjoyed at Sacred Heart. I did not realize how enjoyable those times were until after I left. While I lived at the home, most of my thoughts were bad or negative ones. I just wanted to get away from there. Attending church every day—sometimes three times a day—doing chores, and having no family visits were heavy on my mind. Looking back, the good times did outweigh the bad, but I did not realize it at the time. Now when I reflect on those times, I smile.

My memories of living with the Johnson family were like no others. Living in that family home allowed me to experience many things for the first time. I was allowed to walk to a store and make purchases. I was paid for doing chores. I learned to play piano and to dance. Also I was permitted to watch television almost every day. Those were exciting, interesting, and happy times. My babysitting chore for the Fitzgeralds was the one memory I tried to block from of my mind, but even that was an eye-opening experience. The most important thing I learned from Rev. Fitzgerald was that because a man has the title of "reverend" does not mean he is holy and worthy of my respect. Prior to that time, I believed priests and ministers were men of God who deserved to be on the hierarchal pedestal to heaven. I was immature and did not know any better. Living with the Johnsons prepared me for my life after Sacred Heart.

Suddenly my father's words came back to my mind, marring my memories with thoughts of the past years without a mother or father in my life. From a very young age, I believed my father did not want me. Finally I had received confirmation of that belief. Did he feel the same way about his other children? He divorced his first wife who had five children and then left his second wife who only had one child. Maybe he was afraid of commitment or did not like children. Now I wondered whether I looked like him. The only resemblances I saw between my mother and me were our complexion and hair texture. I was definitely not afraid of commitment, and I loved my children—so those were some things I am glad he and I did not have in common.

Throughout my life, I also believed my mother did not want me. She never gave me reason to believe otherwise. Although many years later my mother and I did develop a relationship, there seemed to be something missing. It was not what I imagined a mother-daughter relationship should be. We were more acquaintances than family. My relationship with Aunt Berenice had been much closer—approximating a mother-daughter relationship. My aunt and I could sit down and talk with each other. She gave me advice she thought I needed, and whenever we met each other, we would hug and kiss. My aunt had even come to Illinois to vacation with me a few times. On the other hand, my mother never had anything good or nice to say to me. No matter what positive things I did or had accomplished, they were never good enough to get a compliment or praise from her. We were finally together yet remained so far apart.

CHAPTER TWENTY-NINE

# WHY WOULD I WANT TO LOCATE MY FATHER?

After that, I drove to Joliet to visit my mother a few times a month, but we never mentioned my father. To my surprise, on a visit several months after she had dropped the bomb of my father's words, she asked, "Have you ever thought about looking for your father?"

After a brief hesitation, I sat back on the sofa in shock—somewhat disturbed that she had asked me that question.

"Before you told me what my father said, there was a slight possibility I would have wanted to locate him, but that possibility vanished. There has not been a day over the past several months that I have not thought about what he said, and I never *will* forget it. I'm not interested in finding him!" I responded. "Why would I look for someone who didn't want me?"

"Well, you have had some time to think about it, so I thought maybe you had changed your mind."

"Why in the world would you think that?" I asked.

"He is your father," she said—as if that was supposed to justify why I should look for him.

"'Father' is just a word to me and nothing more."

She did not respond, so I said abruptly, "If you're interested in finding him, why don't *you* look for him?"

Her face was flushed, and her eyes glazed as she looked at me and said, "Years ago I did try to locate him—without any success."

"Do you really want me to locate him for me—or for you?"

"Both. People change over time," she said. I could not believe what I had just heard.

"Well, I believe if he had changed, he would have tried to locate you or find out what happened to his child. Let's not forget he has other children, so maybe this one did not mean as much to him as the others."

In what I believe to be an attempt to change my train of thought, she said, "This is what I remember about Joe and his family."

Instead of getting up and walking out—which is what I really wanted to do—I sat and listened without interrupting her.

"Joe's father's name is James Cave, and his mother's maiden name was Kathleen Patterson. Your father was short and stocky, and he had squinted eyes. He was the complexion of Baby Joe."

Baby Joe was the nickname we had for one of my grandchildren.

"Your father had six or seven brothers, but I only remember the names James, George, and Eddie. He had five other daughters:

Lucille, Jenny, Emily, Kathleen, and Madeline. He was born in Aiken, South Carolina, and once lived in Augusta, Georgia."

I listened intently without asking questions. I did not comment, because she seemed to be in a talkative mood.

The confusion that her statements created in my head ignited my emotions.

"I still can't understand why you would want to find someone who didn't care whether your child lived or died!" I exploded. "He's not someone I ever want to meet! Why hasn't he looked for me all these years? Evidently he was not interested."

I continued my rant, "Did you abandon me at Sacred Heart because he left you?"

Before she could answer, I added, "Or was it because neither of you wanted me?"

My emotions controlled me. The anger and frustration in my voice was undeniable. My questions were unanswered as I spewed them out so quickly—leaving no room for response.

Before I left her home that day, she handed me a small, beige piece of paper, which I folded without reading and put into my purse. When I got home that evening, I glimpsed at the paper and noticed it contained the information about my father she had told me earlier. I shook my head as I placed it inside of one of my favorite books titled *His Eye Is on the Sparrow*, by Ethel Waters, where it remained for years.

## CHAPTER THIRTY

# MY BIGGEST REGRET

I regret that my mother passed away without my having asked more questions and listened openly to whatever answers were forthcoming. I would have liked to know about her relationship with my father before and after my birth. She told me he left her when I was six weeks old. That makes me wonder why he left his wife and young child. At the time she spoke of him, I was angry and did not want to hear anything more about him. Now I wish I had listened better and asked questions—such as how they met or when they got married or even how long they were married. When she asked me to locate my father, for her sake, I should have tried—even if the search might have been futile.

It took me over forty years to write my mother a letter to ask questions I wanted answered. Most of her answers were not necessarily what I wanted to hear; some questions went unanswered. There were more questions I wish I had asked but did not. I simply neglected to recognize and take advantage of opportunities. Now those opportunities no longer exist, and I can only fault myself for squandering my chances.

My biggest regret is not allowing my mother to hear the word "Mother" from my mouth. At one time she had demanded I call her mother, but I reacted negatively to her efforts at coercion. Her only child robbed her of some aspect of motherhood. I believe that may have caused her everlasting pain. On my mother's birthday and for holidays, I always gave her beautiful cards that contained loving, printed words about motherhood. It had to be difficult for her to read those words but never hear them from me. I gave her many beautiful gifts, but those material gifts could not have meant as much as the verbal one I denied her—which might have been the most precious gift of them all. Many times I gave thought to calling my mother by her first name, but in my mind, that would have been disrespectful. As I look back, I wonder if my not having called her either was even more disrespectful. In my attempt not to disrespect her, I might have done just that.

Though I had never called her "Mother," all of her grandchildren and great-grandchildren called her "Grandma" or "Grandma Pete." Whenever the grandkids saw their grandmother, they hugged and kissed her—which I know meant a lot to her. They loved her just as much as she did them. She knew every one of her great-grandchildren, who at the time of her death numbered fourteen. They loved to visit her, because she always had toys, candy, food, or other material goods for them. She did not waiver when it came to spending money on her great-grandchildren, and they never left her home empty-handed. She bought food as if buying for an army and provided her grandchildren with whatever she thought they might need or want.

I often wondered whether the reason my mother lavished so much love and affection on her grandchildren and great-grandchildren was because she and I lacked those feelings in our relationship. I also tried to make up for my past. I did make a point of regularly telling my children and grandchildren that I loved them. I kept that promise I had made to myself when my children were born that I would never leave them or let them be raised by someone else.

My children and I went through some difficult times, but with prayer, determination, and hard work, we overcame the difficulties and struggles together. There is no substitute for a loving mother-child relationship. As I learned with my own children, a mother-child relationship can be powerful—unsurpassed by any other. I had dreamed of and wished for a relationship like that with my mother, but I believe our stubbornness may have prevented it from happening

## CHAPTER THIRTY-ONE

# MYSTERY OF MY PAST

As an adult, I shifted the blame away from myself to my mother and father. Whom else was I to blame? There might have been a situation or circumstance at fault, but without appropriate documentation, I would never know. One thing was certain: I would never again blame myself for my early childhood experiences. Despite the circumstances, I should never have blamed myself for something over which I had no control. That was a heavy burden for any child to bear. Finally that awful burden was lifted from my shoulders.

Nonetheless, my grown-up self was still frustrated by so many unanswered questions. I embarked on a systematic search for answers. I contacted and received information from Mother Cabrini Home, Inc. The name of the home was changed from Sacred Heart Orphan Asylum to the founder of the home, St. Francis Xavier Cabrini, on

April 12, 1960. Also from the Poughkeepsie Department of Welfare, I obtained information that precisely corroborated what I had learned from Mother Cabrini Home. No reason was documented for my being under their care. Many records had been lost or destroyed.

Finally I discovered—to my amazement—many new details about my childhood. The most surprising information I learned was that the first fourteen years of my life were spent under supervision of the Poughkeepsie Department of Welfare. The documentation I received from Mother Cabrini Home indicated that my mother could not care for me. No further information was available. At the age of three, I had been a patient at Vassar Hospital in Poughkeepsie, New York, for ten days. Hospital records for that time period were no longer available, so I was unable to find out the reason for my hospitalization.

I wrote letters and made phone calls to verify and make sense of my findings. I was determined to learn everything I possibly could about the first thirteen years of my life. Even as I eagerly searched, I was afraid of what I might discover. Nonetheless I kept digging. There were times I thought about discontinuing my efforts, but my desire to know was stronger than the fear of what I might discover. The more I learned, the sadder I became—all the time realizing that my findings were essential for my peace of mind. Finding and amassing that information might have been easier had I started sooner. I could have utilized my mother and other relatives and retrieved information from the agency records.

At some point in my life, I realized I did not remember anything before the age of five, and I became curious about my life before that age. I decided I would try to research as much as possible about those missing years. I contacted the Department of Child Services, schools, and hospitals with very little success. It appeared futile to proceed any further in that particular direction.

I did, however, discover I had been a foster child—not only in one—but four homes before the age of five. When I initially encountered that information, I was angry. Then disbelief took over. I thought I must have read the information incorrectly, so I read it over and over again—hoping the words on that sheet of paper would somehow change. Tears finally prevented me from reading it anymore, but I could not put it away. I sat, stunned, holding that paper in my hands. My anger took over, and I tore it into tiny pieces so that no words would ever be read from it again. However, I knew four years of my life were documented on that paper, which actually had been an index card that was copied onto an eight-and-one-half-by-eleven sheet of paper. The documentation included each family's name and the time I spent at each foster home. Strangely, however, no reason for my being under their care was documented there. Wow, four years of my life documented on one side of a small index card.

The following information was documented on the index card. On December 20, 1947, I was placed in my first foster home (Mrs. Flora McGerald) in Poughkeepsie, New York. On April 6, 1948, I was admitted into Vassar Hospital, where I was hospitalized for ten days. On April 16, 1947, I was placed in another foster home (Mrs. Dyon) and remained there until May 1, 1948. On the day I left Mrs. Dyon's home, I was placed in the foster home of Mrs. McGerald again, where I remained until November 17, 1949. From there, I was placed in the foster home of Mrs. Thelma Yeaden in Ellenville, New York, where I remained until June 21, 1951.

On that date, I was taken by my mother to Sacred Heart Orphan Asylum. It is a mystery as to why my mother, rather than a foster parent or social worker, delivered me. I learned that on April 13, 1955, I had been admitted to Benedictine Hospital, where I was hospitalized for thirteen days. When I was released from the hospital, I was returned to Sacred Heart, where I remained until October 26, 1956. On that date, I was taken to the home of the Johnsons, which was my last foster home. I lived with them for a period of forty-one months. Upon leaving the Johnson family home in May 1959, I thought I was taken back to Sacred Heart only to be placed in another institution, which was Cardinal Hayes Convent Home in Millbrook, New York, where I remained until June 22, 1959. That home is currently known as the Cardinal Hayes Home for Children. That might have been a holding place for me until Sacred Heart had an opening. The reason I had been placed in that institution was never explained to me.

The hospital records for the times I had been admitted were no longer available. Prior to my admission to Vassar Hospital, I had been living in my first foster home and was approximately two years old. I believe my admission to Benedictine Hospital in Kingston might have been due to the injury I received from jumping out of a tree while I resided at Sacred Heart.

Neither my mother nor anyone else in my family ever told me that I had lived in four foster homes prior to Sacred Heart. They should have known, but I had no proof of whether or not they did. If I had known sooner that I had lived in all of those foster homes, I might have asked my relatives why they had not taken me in to live with them. I would have liked to have known the reasons why the first thirteen years of my life were spent living in foster homes and institutions. Maybe it is best that I was too young to remember living in the other foster homes.

The information that was available indicated I was a year old when I was placed into the first foster home. My mother had previously informed me that my father left her when I was six weeks old. The only foster home I was old enough to remember was that of the Johnsons. It was a very good home, where I was treated like a member of their family. At the time I was living there, I did not know it was considered a foster home. I was overwhelmed by what I had discovered.

Suddenly sadness enveloped me. I felt warm and was unable to think coherently—my mind was racing with all kinds of thoughts. My heart was beating so fast that it felt as if it would burst inside my chest. I did not understand what was happening. I felt mentally and physically exhausted. I closed my eyes and took some deep breaths to calm down and gather my thoughts. I could not come up with a reason for my being placed in a foster home—but learning I had been in four was quite disconcerting. If I allowed myself to think of all that happened to me, the rage inside me would explode.

The day I was taken to Sacred Heart Orphan Asylum is clearer in my memory than any other day in my life. When I learned I had spent so much time in foster homes, I felt a profound sense of abandonment. Thinking I was practically given away or not wanted at such an early age made me feel sick in the pit of my stomach. If I had been lovingly adopted, would I have grown into the good, strong person that I am? I will never know. Those placements occurred over forty-five years ago—when I was too young to know what or how to feel. I cannot relive the past, but what I do remember, I have used as a springboard.

The people who welcomed me into their homes when I was too young to understand or even know why or what they were doing for me were precious gifts. They cared for me, fed me, clothed me, and gave me a purpose for being and for staying alive—even though I did not know it at the time.

I have been aware of foster homes most of my life and always have felt there were genuinely caring people who watched over foster children and were honestly concerned about how those children turned out. Also, I know there are foster parents who are uncaring and unfeeling, who have no concern for children, the way they should be raised, or even the way to love them. For some, the foster-care system feeds their greed for money. While money is needed to care for children, that money should not outweigh nurturing of a child. Although during my childhood I did not know what foster homes were or what they were about, I now know that I am very fortunate that God placed me in homes with people who cared and showed me concern and love. Because of the way I turned out, I know that I was blessed at an early age.

# PART IV

# REFLECTION

The only time I returned to Poughkeepsie, New York was to attend my grandmother's funeral in 1987. My mother and I took the train and rented a car when we arrived. This allowed me to visit relatives and Sacred Heart/Mother Cabrini Home. Some of the nuns who were part of my childhood were still there. We reminisced a bit and took pictures.

*Sister Ernesta on a return visit to the home*

*Sister Eleanor and Jo-Ann*

*Jo-ann at Sacred Heart*

*Mother and Jo-Ann at Sacred Heart*

## CHAPTER THIRTY-TW0

# LIFE LESSONS

Reflecting on my life's journey, I realized that I would not be the person I am today without enduring my childhood experiences. My first and most important life lesson—learned from the nuns at Sacred Heart—was faith. A religious upbringing and teachings molded my core. I did not realize at the time that faith would be such an integral part of my life. Prayer is more meaningful in my life today. I say that because I have so much to be thankful for. My faith in God has enabled me to overcome many difficult situations, including the loss of both a child and a husband.

My faith in God supported faith in myself, which has been essential. It allowed me to set goals and believe that I could accomplish them. Once I set a goal, my tenacity would not allow me to quit. I enjoyed school as a young girl but dropped out of high school. However, after the death of my husband left me alone with three children to support, the importance of my education became obvious. The first educational goal I set for myself was to finish high school, which led me to complete a GED program and receive a high school equivalency certificate. Subsequently, I earned a business school program certificate. My employment improved as my education increased, but I realized that a higher education degree would pave the way for success. Thus, I set my educational goals, and they were accomplished.

I was diligent at work, trying to learn as much as possible. Also I was very innovative. I took it upon myself to interview the vice president of one company where I worked to determine what was needed for success. For my personal benefit, I consistently strove to improve my career goals, even though they were difficult to accomplish at times. Each new job was better than the last. I also moved into lateral positions to help me reach my ultimate goal. My studiousness, diligence, and constancy paid off.

I experienced many ups and a few downs during my years of employment. Even when I was fired from a job, I never let it sidetrack me or prevent me from striving for better. Who would ever have thought that my employment history would be so diverse as to include picking vegetables in the fields under the hot Florida sun; doing domestic work; being a bra-factory inspector, a clerk typist, a secretary, a medical transcriber, an administrative assistant, a clerical supervisor, and a center administrator; and, ultimately, being an area administrator overseeing twelve medical clinics in the Chicago area. I did not want to be a person who worked in only one position my entire career. I would not have changed anything. I can honestly say that my employment was versatile, educational, challenging, satisfactory, and fulfilling—both mentally and physically.

My education continued outside of school and the workplace. I joined various organizations and was a museum board member. My mental, physical, and spiritual enrichment also included volunteering. "Giving back" was important to me.

History and geography books held a great interest for me throughout my early school years. From the time I began to study geography and history, I wondered what it would be like to visit another state or a foreign country. Learning about the states in school stimulated a desire to travel. I wanted to see both the well-known attractions and the out-of-the-way, not-so-well-known places.

Reading about the states and actually visiting them were altogether different. I loved to visit as many museums as possible. My travels included visiting twenty-seven of the United States and eight foreign countries. I found that each place had its own uniqueness and held an interesting history lesson. I made it a point when visiting foreign countries to see the beautiful, good, bad, and ugly. Traveling to a foreign country was like entering a new world. I had the opportunity to see and meet people of different cultures and ethnicities in their home environments. My adventures made it possible for me to see how unique various countries are and how the indigenous people live, which was more educational than learning about those places and people from a book.

The realization that I did not have control over everything that happened to me regarding the circumstances of my childhood is another lesson that took some time for me to learn. As a child, I interpreted what I assumed was going on and what I thought was reality. I believe all my early life's challenges, known and unknown, contributed to who I am today. Realizing how well I was treated, how blessed I was, and what the possible alternatives were, I feel spiritually uplifted. This was one of life's lessons from which I have benefitted a great deal.

Another important lesson I learned was that not all mother-daughter relationships are loving. The complexity of the relationship between my mother and me was somewhat detrimental, because it caused both pain and angst. However, I did learn that my emotional reaction to what life brings is up to me. When I am aware of a circumstance, it's up to me to react however I feel is in my best interest at the time. The most important life lesson I learned is forgiveness. Once I forgave, I was able to release the hurtful, negative thoughts and feelings I had carried with me for too many years. When I was able to forgive, my life process became less difficult.

I have learned many important life lessons, one of which is the acceptance of the fact that the world owes me nothing. It took me a long time to learn some of those lessons and reach those conclusions, but I have accepted the things that happened to me and moved on to create my own life.

# EPILOGUE

I give thanks to God every morning I awake to a new day and thank Him for all the yesterdays. Many of those days were filled with happiness or trepidation or both. I am undoubtedly blessed to have lived through those experiences and learned from them. But, without His guidance and my faith and perseverance, that would not have been possible.

My most effective endeavors have been, and will continue to be, driven by passionate desires to achieve. These endeavors of which I speak have allowed me to develop into a mature, strong, and determined woman who will circumvent or traverse detours that might prevent me from reaching my goals. It is my obligation to pursue and enjoy its riches—many of which are not materialistic in nature. My days are brightened with positive thoughts that enhance my mental and spiritual awareness.

The essence of my mental and spiritual existence cannot be measured by accumulated wealth. I have been blessed with riches that far outweigh the material gifts that enhance my daily life, such as: to love and be loved in return; faith to persevere in the face of adversity; and, happiness experienced from some of the smaller nuances of life.

Made in the USA
San Bernardino, CA
16 April 2018